PRAISE FOR GENERATION CHERRY

'*Generation Cherry* absolutely nails   whole
generation who are unable and unwill   lbook,
a battlesuit almost, for all of us who   active
well into our sixties and seventies, an   ....ing to offer the wider
world in terms of experience, stamina and – who knows – possibly wisdom.'

Charles Kingsmill, leading Business Strategy coach

'The great strength of Tim Drake's book about how we should try to come to terms with personal setback in this unwelcome world is that he draws on his own, difficult, experiences of handling a career meltdown… his practical suggestions for dealing with a sudden and painful change in career and personal prospects offer sound guidance not just to older citizens. Many forty plus strivers of today are destined to find the next twenty years a lot harder. They too may find the lessons and coping strategies he has drawn from his experiences not only, and most importantly, practical, but also reassuring and inspiring.'

Stewart Fleming, former US Editor, *Financial Times*

'For those who read this book and identify with its purpose, the third age is one of fulfilment – freed from financial chains they will find purpose and ways to apply it that suit them perfectly. The four autonomies – earning, learning, giving and recharging – give the reader the tools they need to navigate past the obstacles that imprison some in a cynical later life and create the life that they choose.

In an increasingly uncertain and insecure world this is an optimistic and essential guide for our times.'

Malcolm Durham, author of *WealthBeing: a guide to creating wealth and enjoying well-being*

'I think it's brilliant. Packed full of insight, accessible and challenging and a rallying call to make the most of your life at any age.'

Michael Townsend Williams, author of *DO BREATHE: Calm your mind. Find Focus. Get stuff done*

GENERATION CHERRY

Retired?

Redundant?

Rethink!

POWERFUL STRATEGIES
to give you a
SECOND BITE OF THE CHERRY

TIM DRAKE

RedDoor

Published by RedDoor
www.reddoorpublishing.com

ISBN 978-1-910453-20-9

A CIP catalogue record for this book is available from the British Library

Cover design: Clare Turner

Typesetting: Sheer Design & Typesetting

Printed in the UK by Bell and Bain Ltd, Glasgow

To Lizzie, Tansy and Lettice,
who are wonderful, warm, sunny and supportive

CONTENTS

'Everything can be taken from a man but one thing: the last of the human freedoms – to choose one's attitude in any given set of circumstances, to choose one's own way.'

– Dr Viktor E. Frankl
Survivor of Auschwitz, who lost friends, family and his pregnant wife in the concentration camps of World War II

INTRODUCTION

WHAT IS GENERATION CHERRY?

'Lo, life again knocked laughing at the door!'

– Robert Browning

I am part of a privileged generation.

I grew up in the 1950s. At the time we didn't realise we were living in a golden age. Rationing had only just been withdrawn. There was little money around. Or food, or clothing. Foreign holidays were unheard of.

But we understood from our parents that we had survived the war, and things were going to get better.

And they did. Looking back we hit the jackpot in many ways. In comparison to the previous generation, we had a cherry on everything:

- There was no conscription for military service
- We did not have to pay for primary, secondary or tertiary education
- The Beatles, the Stones, Queen and Dylan were fresh and fantastic
- Jobs were plentiful – you could pick and choose
- We benefited from an excellent, free, health service
- The Welfare State was generous, and benefits weren't being cut all the time
- We could afford to buy a house (a big cherry, this)
- We benefited massively from increases in property prices (an even bigger cherry)

- We (well, some of us) had generous work pensions
- There is a state pension which, though not generous, is paid every week.

I speak as a man. Women had smaller – and fewer – cherries. Career opportunities weren't exactly abundant during this time. Many never looked further than being secretaries, teachers or nurses. My wife Lizzie became a nurse, while her brother, similarly talented, became a doctor. Fewer women went to university.

While we have great cause to be profoundly grateful, and the younger generations have reason to be envious (although, to their credit, most of them don't seem to be so), things are no longer entirely rosy.

Restructuring stalks the land, which often means redundancy for experienced, and thus expensive, more mature workers. Many pension schemes have been terminated, or severely watered down. Older workers are not the first choice for job vacancies. End-of-life care-home costs are no longer funded by the state. Increased life expectancy can put stress on those whose savings or pension won't be able to cope.

But looked at from another angle, we live in exciting times. Being healthy and living longer in a more developed and interesting society is a wonderful bonus. It means we are fitting in an extra decade or so to our lives before we even begin to think about getting old.

We can slot in some new adventures or take on some new challenges, especially if the conventional job market has closed its doors to us earlier than we expected.

My own adventures started early, and not through choice. My journey began shortly before my fiftieth birthday, when what had been a gentle cruise towards a successful and comfortable retirement turned into a bit of a whitewater ride. Over the last twenty years since then, I've learned a great deal from the good times, and even more from the not-so-good times.

I found myself in cold and unwelcoming waters, and had to start swimming. Both to save myself, and to support my young family. Good nearly always comes out of bad, and for me it certainly did. So this book contains some of the lessons I've learned, and the insights I've taken from the wisdom and experience of others.

Most important of all, it attempts to define the mindset I have been able to develop in order to take on some of the challenges that face us as we progress through life. These are challenges that are new at this particular time in the evolution of our economy and our society, but they are likely to become more pervasive as the concept of what constitutes work – rather than a job – evolves over time.

WHO IS THIS BOOK FOR?

Who are you, dear reader? For the purposes of this book I am assuming that you have most of the following characteristics:

- You are a human being (very inclusive so far)
- You are in your fifties, sixties, seventies, eighties (possibly your forties or even nineties)
- You are in, or were in, traditional employment (you had a job, ran your own company or were self-employed)
- You either need to, or want to, carry on earning money
- You are full of life and want to spend the time left to you in the most effective, enjoyable and satisfying manner possible.

If my supposition is right, and you fulfil most of these criteria, read on.

WHAT IS A SECOND BITER?

I was on a charity walk on the North Devon section of the coast path with Lizzie. After a mile or so, I fell into step with a lively lady in her mid-sixties. I asked her how she happened to be on the walk. It quickly emerged that she was a relative newcomer to Devon. She and her husband had lived their entire married life in the house in central England he had inherited from his parents. In fact, he had been born in it.

She had been weeding her garden one day when it suddenly struck her that she had been weeding that patch for nearly forty years, and it was quite likely she would weed it till she died. It was an existential moment. And it worried her at a profound level.

Shortly afterwards, their son, who lived close to where we were walking, asked them to move down to be nearer their grandchildren (i.e. help with the babysitting). After prolonged heart searching and discussion, she and her husband decided to do so.

They uprooted, and once in their new home, her husband started a portrait-painting business, something he had wanted to do all his life. And she started to teach pottery, a lifelong interest of hers. Both activities flourished and they now have a very healthy income from doing what they love.

'Do you know,' she said, 'it was like having a second bite of the cherry. We felt years younger, found the grandchildren much more fun and rewarding, and our almost non-existent pension was no longer a problem.' Her only regret was that they hadn't done it years earlier.

As we continued on our walk her words set me thinking. Yes, that's what a lot of people want: a second bite of the cherry. Either when the conventional job market seems closed off to them, or before they even think about retirement. And whatever the stimulus – be it redundancy or retirement – they don't want a future that sees the creative juices dilute, but one where they can flourish, and truly bloom.

So that's what I am. I'm a Second Biter. I started biting a couple or more decades ago, and I want to share some of the benefits – and how to avoid the pitfalls – of taking a second bite.

SO WHAT?

Taking a second bite is more important than ever because we live in a society where the idea of what 'work' entails is changing, and where jobs and therefore redundancy and retirement are evolving as concepts. Jobs are increasingly for those specialists working for large organisations, or for people working in small- and medium-sized companies that have yet to outsource or computerise many of their processes.

While fewer people are being born (global births have been in decline since the 1990s) the global population is growing because more people are living longer. This increasing number of people all need some sort of income for a longer period, both before and after the historically accepted time for their retirement arrives.

And as we live longer, the need to fund living expenses lasts longer. At the same time, medical costs are also increasing relentlessly. All the more so as better and better and more and more expensive medical interventions become available every day – for all stages of life.

There is no doubt that the economics of both de-jobbing and ageing are deeply perplexing. But often overlooked in this popular narrative is the upside – and it's a very big upside – that more and more of us are lucky enough to enjoy reasonably good health for longer.

The economics still demand that something shifts. And this is where it gets exciting. In order to enjoy these golden years (as early as our forties in some cases) we're going to have to take the responsibility for doing so into our own hands.

The goal of this book, therefore, is to persuade you that the glass is considerably more than half-full. And that there is plenty you can do to make it fuller still.

Yes, Generation Cherry is my generation. We've had our cake, eaten it, and can now see we've had a bite of the cherry it had on top all along. Anyone growing up in the 1940s, 1950s, through to the 1970s is part of Generation Cherry.

The cherry may at times look a bit shrivelled, but look closer. It's still full of juice. And there is an appetising second bite awaiting us if we care to take it.

So over the following chapters, we'll work through a strategic approach to the years immediately ahead that will make them satisfying and enjoyable. And at times exciting and fulfilling. It will acknowledge our human frailties but show that we all have the capacity to overcome self-doubt, and to grow as human beings on the journey.

Many of us feel far too young to leave our jobs or retire, and many more of us will find it financially challenging to do so. But the fact we're living longer and in better health is an opportunity to be grabbed.

It's a chance to rethink how we want to spend our time and live our lives.

Whether through choice or necessity we can cast aside concerns about no longer working in a job or being self-

employed. **Not having a job can be a blessing. It can give us the precious opportunity to reassemble our lives so they are more balanced, satisfying and fun.**

IT'S TIME TO TAKE CONTROL!

*'The best time to plant a tree was twenty years ago.
The second best time is now.'*

– Chinese Proverb

CHAPTER ONE

A FRESH MINDSET FOR
A FRESH OPPORTUNITY

This book is about slotting in five, ten, twenty, or perhaps even more years of fully engaged life extension. And taking advantage of trends that might look daunting, but with the right mental approach can be turned to our advantage.

Our first step is to set out the framework needed for the mindset of a successful Second Biter.

The main building block is developing a sense of *autonomy* – of being in control of our lives. It's the foundation for finding fulfilment and happiness in this new, and challenging, stage in our lives. It will give you the confidence and stability to feel good about yourself. It relies on a positive mindset, a strong sense of identity and finding your purpose – all things which could currently be a bit wobbly if you're moving out of traditional employment.

So let's take a preliminary look at these elements to start to flesh out the essential ingredients of the Second Biter.

AUTONOMY – THE FREEDOM TO BE YOU. AND TO BE IN CONTROL

Everything flows back to autonomy: the power or right of self-government. So, in essence, what I'm talking about is taking back control of our lives. Reassembling them in a way that suits us.

In simple terms, we are now the boss. We may well have been the boss when we had a proper job, prior to this change in our life status. But we weren't really.

We had other bosses who pulled our strings. They may have been foreign or domestic owners, or boards of directors, or shareholders, or customers, external bodies or even our staff, before whom we had a strongly felt duty to turn up on time, and behave well, like a leader should.

As a Second Biter, we will have control. Never total control, because we are always answerable to someone – to our partner, our staff, our customers. But more control, because in our new status we can more consciously choose the people with whom, and for whom, we work.

I have worked from home (a great privilege) for more than twenty years, and I can confirm that it is a great feeling to turn down business, or to not work with someone, if you decide not to.

I remember well a time when a client got drunk at an evening business meeting and behaved abominably. It was quite out of character with the person I had previously worked with when sober. I remember both the pain of returning his money to him (I needed it at the time) and the great satisfaction – even relish – of being in control of who I worked with.

The great thing about reaching an age of maturity is that we can fulfil the potential of the promising youngster we have always felt ourselves to be.

It's a chance to be ourselves, and there is all to play for. We may have a sense of dormant potential simmering within us. We may feel a restlessness that just needs encouragement and focus to be productive and fulfilling.

Well, this is our chance. And the first thing to understand is that autonomy is central to achieving what we are looking for.

AUTONOMY IS GOOD FOR US

Research across many studies indicates that autonomy – personal freedom to make our own decisions (*self law* in ancient Greek) – has several benefits:

- It promotes greater conceptual understanding (we are in control and thus more interested in how things work and their likely outcomes).

- It enhances persistence (we own the project or the undertaking and feel more responsible, and committed to a positive outcome).

- It produces greater levels of psychological wellbeing (we are answerable chiefly to ourselves, so we don't need blame-fuelled post-mortems if things go wrong, and we don't have to give away credit if they go right).

- It gives us the dignity of choice. While too much choice can be stressful – especially to young people who understandably have little idea of what they are really looking for – for most people choice is a huge privilege.

A feeling of autonomy will give us confidence that we are in control. And that the future belongs to us. But only if it is accompanied by the right positive mindset.

MINDSET DRIVES EVERYTHING

In the words attributed to Henry Ford, 'If you think you can, or you think you can't, you're right.'

The great opportunity we have in our new economic and demographic context is that there is no template for what to do and how to behave.

There are experts to consult on childbirth and parenting. There is primary, secondary and tertiary education (and beyond) to set us up for our working lives. But there is not much advice around on how to regenerate ourselves to overcome the new financial and psychological challenges caused by unexpected redundancy or skinny, or indeed no, pensions. Which could make our later years considerably less comfortable than we had anticipated. So we have both the need and the opportunity to blast our own path. What is crucial is the mindset we adopt in blasting it.

If you are a glass-half-empty person, there's a risk you will adopt a mindset that sees a future of bleakness, uncomfortable thrift and, as the years pass, an evermore depressing future.

Me, I'm a glass-two-thirds-full person. But in the past I have had moments when the glass looked not only empty but cracked too. So I know it is possible to move from one mindset to the other, and to see it as the chance to rebalance, rethink, re-energise, and have some fun. A different but nevertheless golden period awaits us if we decide to grasp it.

As I alluded to earlier, my personal journey began more than twenty years ago. The company I had built with a partner over fourteen years had been highly regarded by both consumers and the business community alike. But, in the wake of the nineties' recession, it had to be sold in order to protect both our staff and our suppliers.

We succeeded on both fronts, but I personally was left with very little. I was in my fiftieth year, and the script said I would by now be building serious wealth. But we had reinvested our profits in building the business, and taken insignificant salaries and dividends, so I was faced with bringing up a young family with no cash pile and no obvious source of income.

I had an incredibly supportive wife, which took a huge amount of pressure off. And we both had the benefit of having been brought up after the war in homes where thrift was part of our upbringing. My father, who had had to leave school at sixteen to support his mother when his own father died, was a lovely man, but understandably very cost-conscious. We often suggested that he should climb into the fridge and close the door behind him – to be absolutely sure the light was turning off.

Therefore, in a sense, for more than twenty years I have been living the challenge faced by many forty-, fifty- and sixty-year-olds today when they find their work doors closing, their pension and savings prospects threadbare, and no obvious door handles to grasp in front of them.

From personal experience I can confirm that a positive mindset is crucial.

Doubts crowd in after a setback. Self-confidence has understandably taken a hit. There is a strong temptation to give in to dark thoughts. I remember walking along a street near my home shortly after losing my business and seeing a pregnant woman. Because I was preoccupied with my own gloomy situation, I remember thinking 'How can someone think of having a baby at a time like this?' I had to get a grip. I did, and quickly.

The truth is that we can control how we feel, our attitudes and how we approach life in general. The Positive Thinking Industry, with all its exaggerations and excesses, is based on the profound truth that by force of will we can influence our mindset and how we approach life. Many find it easy – or attractive – to mock positive thinking, but the harsh reality is that these people are probably mocking because they are uncomfortable with the logic of being responsible for their own mindset and the impact they have on other human beings.

We are responsible for being positive, uplifting, fun to be with, just as we are responsible for being negative, cynical and a pain to be with. It's a choice we have. In either case, we are responsible.

As the Dalai Lama says, we first of all need to recognise that controlling our feelings and emotions is possible and necessary. We must then recognise that to do so requires considerable effort.

The important outcome for all of us is that finally gaining control of our feelings and attitudes more than justifies that effort.

SELF-WORTH: HOW DO YOU FEEL ABOUT YOURSELF?

It's easy to feel good about yourself when things are going well. You have an important job title, you are part of a strong and winning team, your family and friends look up to you – you are seen as successful.

Even then, there can be moments of doubt. Most people, especially high-fliers, suffer from what is termed Imposter Syndrome. Coined in 1978, this is the term psychologists use to describe the feeling that you really shouldn't be in the position of importance or authority you find yourself in, and that you are about to be found out.

It's the feeling you get in a situation where anxiety starts to build because you are sure you are about to be exposed and unmasked: 'I'm not as bright, talented, experienced, wise, innovative (fill in the blank) as people think I am'.

It is very natural, and it is very widespread. Psychologists estimate that about three quarters of people suffer from it. And the other 25 per cent are either narcissistic, insensitive or unhealthily self-confident.

The time: 22 November 2003. The place: Telstra stadium, Sydney, Australia. The event: the Rugby World Cup Final. The match, between traditional foes – England and Australia – is tense, incredibly tense. At full-time the match is drawn, and goes to extra time. Extra time piles pressure on pressure. It is 17–17 with thirty seconds to go.

The England forwards pile down the field towards the Australian line following a darting break by their scrum half, Matt Dawson. The ball comes back to Jonny Wilkinson, who stays ice-cool under the pressure. He drops a goal, to win the game 20–17. The crowd goes wild, and even the Australian fans stand to applaud him.

Jonny was already a global icon in the game of rugby. He continued playing at the highest level for another eleven years, transforming the position he played in. When he started his seventeen-year career, players in his position – fly half – were expected to kick, run and direct operations, but were not expected to tackle large and aggressive opponents too often. Jonny not only kicked, ran and directed operations brilliantly, but he tackled with real aggression, frequently sending much larger opponents flying backwards.

Jonny became a legend, and in the last two years of his career played for the French team Toulon, which he captained and led to European Cup victory two years running. The Toulon team was made up of top internationals from around the world – from South Africa, England, Australia, and even a couple from France.

All these great players spoke in awed terms of Jonny's qualities as a player, and as a captain and a human being.

This is what Jonny said after the second European Cup Final triumph in 2014, on the eve of his retirement at the age of thirty-five, having scored 13 of the total of 23–6 point victory, and having received a standing ovation from the entire crowd: 'I have been given too much respect and others deserve it more. *Some will realise soon I am a bit of a fraud.* I have been part of great teams and others should get the credit.'

Fear and self-doubt afflict us all. So if they afflict you, there is no need to feel alone. It is not you that is inadequate. It's just part of being human, and it doesn't go away with increased age. If you haven't suffered from it recently don't be surprised or downhearted if it comes upon you suddenly as things begin to change in your life.

But how can we prepare for and combat it?

THE IDENTITY QUESTION

Addressing the question to someone of mature years at first sight might look a bit odd. But it's very relevant.

The question 'What do you do?' is often the one we first encounter when meeting new people. It can be a challenging question to face if for many years you have confidently responded, 'I am a [xxxx]'.

Not knowing how to answer *what* you are can quickly lead to self-questioning of *who* you are.

Let's look at both of them.

WHAT ARE YOU?

It's a question that applies as much to teachers or public servants as it does to business leaders or senior management – it affects people in all walks of life. I've known lots of high-fliers who defined themselves by how many people reported to them, or by the turnover or scope of their department or company. But when this comes to an end they've been left bereft. The sudden loss in status has them looking for the oxygen mask.

And redundancy or retirement, in any form, is no different. Our job title, whatever it was, has gone. How do we describe ourselves? Who are we?

'I was a doctor/administrator/businessman/businesswoman' is straightforward. Shifting to, 'I have a portfolio of interests' or 'I'm plural' can take time to adjust to. It's difficult to explain, especially if we ourselves are unsure of what it actually means. **We can become hypersensitive to what people think of us.** A sense of paranoia can easily creep in, and a feeling the look you receive in response is really saying, 'Oh yes, you're old/you've no longer got a job/ you're struggling.'

If you're not clear what role you are playing in life, it's easy for your self-confidence to take a knock – it's tough to convince yourself let alone anyone else that you are a valuable person of depth and substance.

This element of self-perception in our status – how important our own view of our 'title' is – has recently been highlighted dramatically by three German academics. In a study written up in the *Economic Journal*, Hetschko, Knabe and Schöb found that people going directly from unemployment benefit to a pension felt a dramatic improvement in their sense of wellbeing. The label 'retired' or 'pensioner' was a far better identity with which to face the world than 'unemployed'.

And it's no different when we move on from what we are now. Coming from being a manager/leader/scientist/lawyer to 'redundant' or 'retired' can be a tough change to take. You are no longer 'a [fill in the blank]' but out of work or a senior citizen.

This is totally understandable but far too often under – or not – prepared for. Building a strong sense of identity – over and above a job title or description – is vital in order to foster and preserve a positive sense of self-worth to ride this stormy time. A strong sense of identity protects a robust self-confidence.

WHO ARE YOU?

We've seen the dangers of relying on 'what' you do for a sense of identity. During redundancy or retirement this comes sharply into focus and it links directly into 'who' you feel you are. It's important to understand as it goes directly to the heart of feeling confident and having the power to be autonomous. It is the lynchpin to getting a second bite of the cherry.

Who are you? The answer is hopefully both plural and mobile. Plural because we all have multiple identities around a central core. And mobile because as we grow and develop, and as circumstances around us change, so too will the elements of our identity readjust themselves.

Our multiple, mobile identities will include roles and interests. Roles like entrepreneur, team player, innovator, boss/worker, aunt/uncle, mother/father, son/daughter, trustee, committee member, coach, mentor, friend, party-goer, and a whole lot more besides. You may belong to a social club, support a football team, be a keen stamp collector, a wildlife enthusiast, or strongly support a particular political party – all of these interests play a part in your identity, too. These varying titles are a necessary part of being a social human being and bring richness to our identity.

But hitting retirement or redundancy, and its potential knock to self-confidence can, if you're not careful, see the breadth of your identity dwindle. You're feeling low; you can quickly start seeing fewer people. Or perhaps you withdraw from the world to indulge in some downtime; you've earned it after all. But you might see your wider interests shrink as a result, and your identity with it. Quite soon, you've got very little to talk about other than the weather.

And diluting down to a singular identity is also potentially precarious. Becoming a carer for a loved one, for example. Nursing our dying partner, we find our whole being taken up with the task. Such dedication is to be greatly admired, but it is still worth devoting what cracks of time are available to sustain other elements of who we are. Otherwise it could make re-engaging with everyday human society even more challenging, once the period of shared suffering comes to a close.

But perhaps you're firing on all cylinders. Retirement is newly yours and you are raring to use your time wisely. It's why you bought the book. Your identity is boasting plurality and is happily mobile. It is unlikely you'll be morphing personalities on a regular basis, but you may be playing several roles that require you to present a slightly different side of yourself to the world, depending on the situation.

A word of warning, though: Nurturing our multiple identities can also be a challenge.

Adolescence is a classic period of multiple personalities – trying out different personae in search of what most accurately reflects our inner stage of evolution.

The risk of too much morphing, and too often, is that we can become less at ease in new social situations. Chopping and changing facets of our personalities can leave us in danger of becoming panicked or stressed by unfamiliar settings and people, as we scramble to assemble the parts of our character best suited to the situation. Better to avoid these dangers by maintaining more consistency across the varying roles you may play, ensuring your social pathways remain open.

The way to retain and navigate your various roles in a healthy way, with confidence, is to act from a strong base – your essential core.

We all know someone whose self-confidence is ebbing. They act out of character, they parrot what other people say, they have little to say for themselves. Quite simply, they are not acting themselves. Their behaviour is out of whack with their essence. They've forgotten their inner sense of self.

Integrity is all. And it needs reaffirming regularly.

Beyond its crucial role of underpinning your broader sense of identity, it is *morally right* to be true to yourself, and not to mould yourself to the views or demands of the last person you spoke to.

What's more, this situational ethic – being sucked into the values of those around you – can be *psychologically* very damaging. Having different values, and a different personality, at home from those you espouse at work for example, is pretty destructive. Both to your peace of mind and to your sense of self-worth. Your conscience – a concept validated over all cultures and across all times – knows who you are. It can't be fooled, and attempts to do so can lead to considerable stress and a whittling away at self-confidence.

Finally, it's worth being aware that tribalism can put your core integrity under pressure. Our interests see us belonging to different tribes, and most of us belong to several. Our nationality is one tribe. Our religion may be another. Being a Muslim or a Christian may be extremely important to you. Within that, being a Shia or a Sunni, or a Catholic or a Protestant, may be even more important.

You may belong to a social club, support a football team, be a keen stamp collector, a wildlife enthusiast, or strongly support a particular political party. The level of engagement may vary between the tribes you belong to, but if you meet someone from the same tribe, you will engage with them easily and immediately find common ground.

But tribalism can be potentially destructive, if it leads you to views or behaviours that contradict who you are as a human being. I love sport. Both doing it and attending sporting events. But I have witnessed fans behaving in ways totally at odds with their normal belief systems. They say and do things that they would find abhorrent if they saw other people doing them in the cold light of day. And it's not just about alcohol-induced madness, it's about subjugating oneself to the norms of the tribe and the dangers of a pack mentality. **So your central core, your personal integrity, can easily be put under strain. Therefore it's vital to have a grounded sense of self. It gives you a self-confidence that can help ensure the social pathways remain open and your multiple identities continue to chime and flourish.**

Being, like me, a Second Biter is a very useful identity to have. But to underpin the identity and make it sing, it will need to be built on the sound foundation that comes from a sense of autonomy and a positive mindset.

We need to feel good about ourselves. To be proactive and to feel in control. When we can achieve this, the cherry that defines our generation will once more look very appetising. And we'll enjoy each bite.

CHAPTER TWO

WHAT TO DO – THE FOUR AUTONOMIES MINDSET

Anyone who has been in any commercial or professional walk of life knows the importance of case histories, and how they work. The case history demonstrates the journey of your organisation to new employees, potential investors, important visitors, stakeholders, bankers and anyone else that needs to be informed or influenced to think well of you.

It's usually a good story, and success from the start is made to look inevitable and well deserved. In fact, case histories are nearly always a massive tidying up of what was in reality a very messy journey in which serendipity played a large role. Post-rationalisation is the name of the game. The facts are made to fit the final outcome; it is made to look as though there was not a moment of doubt along the way.

The strategy I am about to set out does, like all case histories, involve some post-rationalisation. But the four elements we're going to focus on were all there for me twenty-plus years ago, even though I couldn't see them clearly at the time. They were instinctive rather than rational, and none the worse for that.

The strategy involves adopting a mindset that revolves around four core autonomies. Four autonomies that will see you become the boss. You'll be deciding how to run your life. What I am talking about is taking control – and more importantly *feeling* in control – of what we do with our lives.

The Four Autonomies Mindset allows us to become leaders. We are Leaders of Our Lives, rather than just passively living our lives. And by initiating and directing what we do with our days, we not only gain control but also incredible fulfilment.

Each of the four autonomies is individually important. And their effectiveness is hugely enhanced when operated together. They focus on:

- Earning
- Learning
- Giving
- Recharging.

THE BENEFITS TO YOU OF THE FOUR AUTONOMIES

Each of the four autonomies has enormous benefits. It is no understatement to say that they can be transformative for your effectiveness as a human being. Not only that, but you'll also be much happier as a person when you master them. Here they are, with their benefits:

- **Earning.** Even if you have a work pension or extensive savings you may still need extra income to make life comfortable. If you have a skinny pension, or none, or have lost your income unexpectedly, earning will be a powerful imperative. Earning – even a modest amount, for a very few hours a week – also has the benefit of keeping you connected to work in general – and therefore what is going on in the society in which you live. You stay plugged into the minds of the people who are still actively involved in the workplace.

- **Learning.** Everyone needs to learn, so they are growing rather than wilting. Keeping the mind engaged, continually being topped up, or just functioning well, is crucial to staying actively involved in life. Once we stop learning we are effectively accepting that we are treading water until we die. Learning engages us in life, it is fun, and fulfilling.

- **Giving.** Giving back, in the form of volunteering, caring, or sharing experience and wisdom, is immensely rewarding psychologically. It means you are participating. You are a player in the game of life. And it strengthens your self-worth at a time when it might wobble. And, yes, it keeps you human.

- **Recharging.** Sport, hobbies, travel, the arts, entertainment and socialising are both engaging and enjoyable. They are relaxing and have the effect of recharging our batteries. Like a mobile phone, if you don't recharge it, it's not a lot of use. Recreation re-creates us. You'll have a great time, and get fresh energy in the process.

THE BENEFITS TO SOCIETY OF THE FOUR AUTONOMIES

Not only do the autonomies create benefits for you, they create benefits for society as a whole. So it's a profound win/win all round. Here they are in all their glory:

- **Earning.** Continuing some form of work can mean you are paying tax, and thus helping the health and welfare of your fellow citizens. You are also helping in a very real sense to improve the dependency ratio – the number of working people to the number of those dependent on tax revenues: the sick, the very young and those subsisting on welfare or state pensions.

- **Learning.** Continuing to develop yourself means you can be more rounded and effective in your work, and thus contribute more. You can also be more productive in your giving back because your wisdom and insight will be constantly refreshed and updated.

- **Giving.** Through volunteering, caring and doing worthwhile unpaid work you are helping the social sector in society, which is in increasing need of your support. And because research proves that volunteers tend to be healthier, happier and more active, you are therefore making fewer demands on the physical and mental health budgets that are sorely overstretched and need all the help they can get.

- **Recharging.** Travelling, eating out, taking part in sporting or entertainment events often means you are not only having fun but also spending money, and thus contributing to the economy. Spending money means more jobs, and a healthier society.

Let's have a look at each one in turn and see how they work. Each autonomy will be explored in its own chapter and each chapter will begin with one of 'Seven Insidious Excuses forcefully rejected by highly effective people'. These excuses are reasons we use to get out of doing things that feel a little tough. We need to reject these justifications for inaction and realise they're just procrastinations, false-exemptions and excuses.

But before we get to the four autonomies, let's do an important mental warm-up exercise. This involves applying some basic common sense to our day-to-day material needs.

It means engaging with the possibility of having less stuff – and possibly less money – in a positive way, a way that understands that thrift needn't be disabling. Indeed, it can be liberating.

CHAPTER THREE

WARMING UP FOR AUTONOMY WITH ENLIGHTENED THRIFT

'He who will not economise will have to agonise'.

– Confucius

Enlightened Thrift – the ability to enjoy and benefit from living on less – is a way of life. It is also a vital building block to put in place in order to develop the **Four Autonomies Mindset**.

For those who are comfortably off, and well upholstered with significant financial assets, and a good pension – good luck and well done. For the rest of us, re-learning the values of thrift can be both cleansing and uplifting.

So if it's not relevant to you, you hereby have an excuse to skip this chapter. For those with a less assured safety net, read on …

THE CULTURAL CONTEXT OF WEALTH AND THRIFT

As we will see in the next chapter, historically wealth meant something much wider than just the financial definition we understand today.

For centuries, in Imperial China the literati were revered not for their financial assets, but for the intellectual and spiritual wealth they had built up from their pursuit of knowledge and cultivation of the arts. They spent their time memorising the Confucian classics rather than acquiring money and possessions.

In traditional Jewish communities, studying the Torah was seen as a superior way of life to the acquisition of money. Monks, Buddhist or Christian, see poverty as a moral imperative. Indeed, a life of privation – the absence of the vulgarities often associated with financial wealth – and a duty to give to the poor, have for centuries across different cultures been seen as highly desirable attributes in an evolved and civilised society.

So it is nothing new or out of the ordinary to view thrift – consciously consuming only what is necessary, and editing out anything that is unnecessary or vulgarly frivolous – as an enlightened, almost noble, way of life.

Thrift is an interesting word. It comes from the word **thrive**, and in the sixteenth and seventeenth centuries it meant *prosperity* – something or someone that was flourishing, worthy, fortunate. It also had the more modern sense of *frugality* – being provident and economical. The word carried both senses until more recent times, when the frugality aspect came to dominate.

Enlightened Thrift is old-style thrift. It is about prosperity *alongside* frugality.

I learned this lesson from a chastening personal experience. As I mentioned at the beginning of the book, I was approaching fifty when the company I had co-founded and built successfully over fourteen years had to be sold for very little indeed to protect staff, suppliers and customers.

Traumatic as it was, it did solve one problem. During my forties, when the company was doing well, our bankers had valued my personal shareholding in the millions. As a result, I had been having a constant debate with my wife, Lizzie. The debate centred on how we would instil in our two children the value of money.

We had both been brought up in the post-World War II economy, in loving families that had very little money to spare. A perspective of the relative tightness of money in relation to today's economy comes from Andrew Dilnot, chair of the UK Statistics Authority.

He recently estimated that the average UK income in the late 1930s (*before* the devastating impact of the war on the economy) was **20 per cent of the average income today** – with prices of everything staying the same. This means if you were earning an average income, **your spending power would be one fifth** of what it is today. Whatever job you are in – or were in – imagine living on 20 per cent of that income.

So until our late teens, when things started to improve slowly, we never ate out, or went on foreign holidays. But things weren't tough – they were just tight. Our expectations were lower, and we therefore appreciated small gifts and treats more intensely than most of today's children.

Clothes were hand-me-downs and seldom fitted properly. But with everyone in the same boat, it didn't seem to matter. Some pieces of clothing were more embarrassing than others, of course, but we all just got on with it.

This meant there was little sense of entitlement, and, in the early days, keeping up with the Joneses next door was irrelevant as the Joneses were just getting by, too.

This world of communal romantic privation began to dissolve when the factories of the Western powers stopped making guns, tanks and aircraft, and started making consumer goods for consumption by increasingly well-remunerated workforces.

Envy is a powerful and insidious motivator, and as Vance Packard showed in his seminal book *Hidden Persuaders*, marketers used it very effectively to advertise and sell increasing amounts of goods as the US economy bounced back quickly in the postwar years. The UK and Europe crawled back, rather than bounced back, so Lizzie and I were fortunate in having been brought up at a time before people jockeyed for superiority with the size of their house, or their television screen. Social inequality was lower – there was a feeling that everyone was in it together. We hadn't had many *things*, and we hadn't felt at a competitive disadvantage for not having had them.

Our sudden dramatic fall in income – and the virtual disappearance of our potential pension with the demise of the company – was sobering, but not as sobering as it might have been, had we not had an upbringing of what we could now see was healthy thrift.

It was complicated, of course, by the fact that we were responsible for our two daughters – then aged six and ten. But our initial concern at the situation was much mitigated by the realisation that the challenge we were facing over how to instil in them the value of money had been solved. We were no longer role-playing. This was the real thing.

The strange fact was that we came to enjoy it – even relish it. Just as people who win the lottery often rapidly spend themselves poor again, we were back in the relative financial comfort zone of the thrift of our younger years. We had – in the words of the wartime slogan that endured for many years after the war was over – to make do and mend.

The happy outcome was that our two girls took to it like ducks to water. They were comfortable being less well off than some of their friends, and very seldom pestered us for material things. Also, they had the self-confidence to say no if better-off friends invited them to restaurants or outings that were beyond their means.

And to this day – though relatively successful in their work – they still buy many of their clothes in second-hand shops. Indeed, it is Enlightened Thrift in action. They could probably afford more expensive things – clothing, entertainment or cars – but they choose not to. They travel almost everywhere by bicycle, and they share a clapped-out car which has an extremely low financial value.

Money is not a motivator for them. Which is just as well, as most of their friends are neither lawyers, accountants, bankers nor in corporate jobs that pay high salaries. Their friends are talented – often doing creative or worthwhile jobs in the caring industries, or starting out as entrepreneurs – but not in highly rewarded occupations.

No one, of course, can tell what might have happened had we today been financially wealthy and the girls been brought up in an environment where money was no object. What I can say is that Lizzie and I are very pleased we didn't have to take the risk.

THE BENEFITS OF ENLIGHTENED THRIFT

Since the recession that began in 2008, Enlightened Thrift – prosperity with frugality – has been a course of action that more and more people are following. An awareness of how stretched most national economies are, coupled with experience at first- or second-hand of how vulnerable employment is, means a lot of people have reduced both their spending and their debt.

Whether a conscious decision to spend less, or a necessity forced upon them, there are benefits to Enlightened Thrift. Here are a few of them:

- It strengthens your autonomy before you even start on the Four Autonomies Mindset – giving you that solid base to begin from.
- It makes you realise you have choices and that in turn reduces fear.
- Not spending creates more potential prosperity to go with the frugality and can foster a sense of peace, gratitude and a spirit of generosity.
- Concurrently, spending less on kids' toys or entertainment is shown by research to create a closer bond with children than those whose relationships are more, in sociologist speak, 'mediated by objects'. A double win – less unnecessary consumption, and potentially better relationships with children and grandchildren.

- It can reduce the potential for friends – or families – to drift apart because of differences in spending power.
- It builds self-confidence – you are taking control of your finances.
- It keeps you in touch with what things cost, and thus what is happening in the real economy.
- It can create more insight into, and sympathy for, those living lives of financial desperation.
- It is better for the planet. Consuming less by definition implies a reduced consumption of scarce resources such as fossil fuels or other sources of energy.

KEEPING UP WITH THE JONESES.
UNDERSTANDING MONEY AND ITS PLACE IN OUR LIVES

Feeling dissatisfaction with our lot reduces our autonomy and therefore weakens our starting position for the Four Autonomies Mindset.

Compared to someone living an agricultural life in a village in, say, the Indian sub-continent, most people reading this book are very wealthy indeed. But that remote comparison doesn't tend to filter into our day-to-day understanding of how well off we feel.

Most of us don't live in absolute poverty. We may be less well off than we would like to be in absolute terms, but *it's the direct comparisons that undo us.*

Luke Johnson, a serial and successful entrepreneur in the UK, tells the story of a friend of his, whose father had become seriously unhappy. The friend's father had been a successful banker, with a large home, a ski chalet and all the trappings of significant financial wealth of a senior person in his line of business. He had then made the mistake of taking over the private client side of the banking operation, where he was dealing with the uber-rich, with their private jets, fleets of cars and private islands. The *power of association* kicked in. In no time at all he felt financially unsuccessful, vulnerable and unhappy.

'You can tell what God thinks of money by the people he gives it to'

– Dorothy Parker

The widespread human need to compare and feel equal or superior as a result of the comparison isn't anything new. 'Keeping up with the Joneses' was a well-known phenomenon coined in the boom of consumerism in the 1960s. And it was acknowledged long before that during the 1920s Depression, in the famous *New Yorker* cartoon: a man is in his boss's office and has obviously just had his request for a rise in salary turned down. The caption reads: 'I understand I can't have a rise, but could everyone else have a pay cut?'

Financial wealth comparison is so powerful because it is founded in the age-old sin of envy. The envy is often supercharged by inequality. If everyone is in it together – as after World War II – envy is less of an issue. But in unequal societies – as many of ours have become – the desire is intensified not only to have what the other person has, but to have *more*. Enough is not enough.

This is understandable – it's a basic human emotion – but in the context of Second Biters, the problem is that it's just plain stupid. It is stupid because in comparing yourself to others and feeling envy, you are disempowering yourself. You are handing over power to other people. Directly or indirectly, they are controlling how *you* think and feel.

Fundamentally, you are giving up autonomy. Which, of course, is counterproductive if your goal is to develop the four autonomies that will give you a rewarding and fulfilling second bite of the cherry.

*'At the end of the day, dignity is more important
to the human spirit than wealth'*

– Jacqueline Novogratz, CEO Acumen, talking about poverty

THERE'S PLENTY TO GO AROUND

The concept of the Abundance Mindset was first outlined by Stephen Covey, one of the greats of personal and professional development, in *The 7 Habits of Highly Effective People.* The basic idea is that there are enough resources and successes around for everyone to have their share. Its opposite, the Scarcity Mindset, posits that there is insufficient of either, and therefore everyone is in competition with everyone else for what little there is.

Abundance Mindset says there is plenty to go around, so win/win in human negotiation is both possible and desirable.

Scarcity Mindset says it's a zero sum game. The cake is of a finite size, so fight to get the biggest slice for yourself, and the devil take the hindmost.

Mark Twain nailed the Scarcity Mindset, with its propensity to assume the worst outcomes from any given situation, when he wrote: 'My life has been filled with terrible misfortunes. Most of which have never happened.'

As Second Biters, what can we learn from Stephen Covey and his Abundance Mindset?

First, it enables you to recognise that you have *choices*. Both in how you *feel* about the situation, and in what decisions you actually make. There are lots of ways you can approach your situation on a financial dimension. At one extreme you could spend like mad, and trust you die before the money runs out or you win the lottery. Or you could follow a path of Enlightened Thrift, and have a good chance of enjoying the journey to the hereafter, however long it might be.

Second, because you know you have choices, it *reduces fear*. Fear is unproductive, and limits your ability to operate effectively. It closes down even the most open of minds. But because you know you have several courses of action, many of which will bear fruit, you are less fearful, and more relaxed. Abundance of options means you can take risks. Even if you fail, there will still be options available, you will have learned. And upsides will still be available.

Finally, recognising that there's enough to go around fosters a perspective of *gratitude*. You appreciate how much you have, and as a result you can take pleasure in being generous to others. Not spraying gifts around like confetti, but sharing money and time with worthwhile causes, small and large, including your loved ones. The fear is reduced, the endorphins are released, and the Helpers' High (see Chapter 6) can be yours.

Of course, it makes sense to associate with people who also have an Abundance Mindset. You don't want your choices reduced by those with a Scarcity Mindset, who are themselves fearful and will encourage you to be the same. Especially those who may seek to make you feel inadequate because you can't keep pace with their lifestyle.

Fear is infectious. Like negativity in general, shun people who have it. And validate your autonomy by taking responsibility, shifting your perspective and realising that there is enough for everyone. It's not a zero-sum world.

ENOUGH IS ENOUGH

There is a story, possibly apocryphal, of two American writers, Joseph Heller and Kurt Vonnegut, at the party of a billionaire in Los Angeles. Having nosed around the mansion, with its swimming pools, indoor and outdoor cinemas, bars and gold-plated everything, Heller says to Vonnegut, 'Gee, this guy has everything!' To which Vonnegut replies, 'We have one thing this guy will never have.' 'What's that?' asks Heller. To which the answer is, 'Enough.'

Enough, for a Second Biter, is both a psychological and an emotional concept.

'The world is too much with us; late and soon, Getting and spending, we lay waste our powers: We have given away our hearts, a sordid boon!'

– William Wordsworth, 1804

Wordsworth, the great Romantic poet, wrote these lines over 200 years ago, and they go to the heart of why Enlightened Thrift is so necessary. Modern society (what Wordsworth elsewhere memorably called, 'this disease of modern life') has a built-in dynamic that says *more is good.*

Psychologically, we feel just that little bit more financial wealth would make all the difference. We'd feel better about ourselves – we would have made it to a point of financial stability where we could relax. Emotionally, the element of fear would have finally been contained, and our anxiety about our financial vulnerability would have been turned down to an acceptable level.

Study after study recording people's feelings about how much money they need to be happy show that the answer is a bit more than they already have, regardless of how much they have or earn. That little bit extra income would make all the difference to their happiness. The goal of financial nirvana is always on the horizon, always moving away.

Not only do we never achieve it, we damage ourselves in the attempt. As Wordsworth says, we are getting and spending all the time, so we lay waste our powers. We lay waste our powers of engaging with others in a generous and wholehearted way. Our powers of giving back, of growing, and fulfilling our purpose.

We are in danger of giving away our hearts to achieve the sordid boon of achieving more – probably unnecessary – financial wealth.

Enlightened Thrift enables you to blow the whistle on this self-destructive getting and spending.

'If I can only scrape a living, at least it's a living worth scraping'

– Mickey Smith, The DO Lectures, Wales 2011

THRIFTY THINKING AVOIDS FEAR AND PROMOTES EMPATHY

The Roman philosopher Seneca the Younger (c. 4 BC–AD 65) led a colourful life, despite his Stoic philosophy. For him, an important element in stoicism was the necessity to confront fears, and by facing them, to overcome them.

As a result he lived an early version of Enlightened Thrift (despite rumours of living more than comfortably for the rest of the time). His advice is well worth thinking about as a potentially effective way to neutralise our worst fears of economic deprivation:

'Set aside a number of days each month where you are satisfied with the cheapest and scantiest of fare (food) and the roughest of dress, all the while asking yourself "Is this the condition I fear?"'

And Thrifty thinking doesn't just reduce overheads; it promotes empathy. If you are lucky enough in your later years to be in a well-upholstered financial position, good on you, but there is a danger in your situation. That danger is your becoming – to a greater or lesser degree – emotionally distanced from the mainstream of life, as well as from your family and friends.

Your strong finances may mean you are cosseted, in a comfort zone of financial privilege. You are at a remove from the real world because money – and especially the discomfort of the lack of it – has lost its meaning for you. Intellectually, you understand its importance and role in the world of day-to-day existence, but it is through a lens that distorts.

You are mentally living in a gated community, from which the majority of your fellow humans are excluded. You may think you understand and sympathise, but it is at a comfortable distance.

Practising Enlightened Thrift enables your powers of empathy to be more finely tuned, and more frequently engaged. You are constantly feeling what it is like to go without, to make do, to live like the majority of the human race. Taking public transport home (if it's available) after a night out, rather than a taxi, I can tell you from frequent personal experience, keeps you healthily plugged in. And often entertained by the high spirits of fellow passengers. You are sharing human experiences, rather than witnessing them as a spectator. You are engaged with life around you, rather than living at a remove from it.

Whether to go for distance or proximity is an important choice for you. Going for Enlightened Thrift helps you bite on the cherry, rather than just sucking on it.

ENLIGHTENED THRIFT CAN BRING RECOGNITION

In 1759, France began the Seven Years' War against Britain. The war spread across many areas of the globe, and by its end Britain had won several colonies in North America and the West Indies from the French. Financing the war was a problem for France, and in 1759 the job of raising the money was given to Etienne de Silhouette.

Silhouette took the job seriously, and not only reduced the spending of the Royal Household but set about taxing the rich.

As a result, he didn't last long in the job, and retired to his chateau amid great ridicule. At the time, a simple art form was emerging – the black shadow profile set against a white background – which was simple and inexpensive. The French nobility mocked it, and gave it the name of a Silhouette to dramatise its cheeseparing characteristic.

This tale symbolises two aspects of Enlightened Thrift. First, the good sense of rigorous, brave and enlightened budget control, demonstrated by Silhouette (his absence damaged the French cause). Second, the ability to live, with style, on less. The silhouette is a portrait of an individual or individuals that has retained beauty, quality and impact, at a price well below that of a painting or a sculpture. Bravo for Etienne!

WHAT'S THE PLAN?

I obviously don't know your current financial situation, so you will have to adapt the following to suit your circumstances. The goal is to develop your own plan to help you adopt a life of Enlightened Thrift.

As Robert Kiyosaki, the author of the *Rich Dad, Poor Dad* book, has pointed out, rich people tend to buy assets, while poor and middle-income people tend to buy liabilities – *and think they are assets*. Over the long term, assets increase your wealth, whereas liabilities deplete it.

It is probable that your years of peak earnings are no longer ahead of you (though hopefully they might be). So you are where you are, and have to make the best possible fist of it you can.

The problem for most middle-income earners – and even higher-income earners – is that income and expenditure have tended to run neck and neck through their lives. More often than not, expenditure has run slightly in the lead. Costs increase as families grow up, but they also increase because of the understandable societal pressures to have *more*.

A bigger house or a bigger car may look like a necessity for a growing family, but it's probably not. A bigger car or house might also be perceived as a necessary adjunct to a more senior role at work, but that's vanity – understandable but not good sense.

A bigger house can be considered an asset if the property prices in your area are going up, and may be a good idea, but the higher mortgage is likely to reduce spending power. Worse, you are paying out dead money to service interest on the higher debt. If property prices are static or declining, it becomes a liability rather than an asset. If interest rates go up, the cost of the liability increases, putting further pressure on disposable income.

A bigger car, especially one that is regularly updated to a newer model, creates more damage to your financial wealth by adding to the liability side of the balance sheet. It is rapidly reducing in value, and you are stuck with the payments every month. Even if you do finally own it, the value of the asset is likely to have at least halved in value.

The same goes for most of the stuff we accumulate, from tennis rackets, golf clubs and expensive clothes to foreign holidays we can't really afford. They are all liabilities, and detract, rather than add to, our balance sheet. They also reduce income, and if bought on credit, deplete future income.

I'm not suggesting that we never treat ourselves to anything. Just that we think at least twice about whether we really need it, or, considering a policy of Enlightened Thrift, ask ourselves whether it is just an indulgent vanity that adds no real value to the quality of our lives.

SECOND BITER BALANCE SHEET

So you might consider looking at your overall assets and liabilities in the form of a Balance Sheet. This sounds a bit mechanistic – and it is – but it might provide some insights into your financial situation, so you can make more informed decisions on what actions you might take.

Obviously, all assets come with risks. Illness, war or serious social unrest can decimate the value of most assets – especially shares or property. But assuming a reasonable degree of social stability and economic growth, the following might make up the core of your low risk financial assets:

- Property – your primary residence
- Property – second home, or let
- Stocks and shares
- Your pension fund – company and/or private
- Collections – art, rare books, stamps, vintage cars – (higher value fluctuation/risk)
- Cash – in bank or hand.

Possible income streams could include:

- Part- or full-time job
- Income from pension (see above)
- State pension (small but reliable)

- Dividends on shares
- Income from rented property
- Interest on cash in bank
- Annuities
- Entrepreneurial activities.

And don't forget the gig economy (see Chapter 4 for more detail). It's easier than ever to become a micro-entrepreneur at low risk by using specialised websites. Here are a few to consider:

- Become an artisan retailer selling the objects you make (clothing, accessories, jewellery) via a marketplace such as Etsy
- Become a part-time hotelier through Airbnb or onefinestay
- Sell your particular expertise(s) on TaskRabbit
- Convert dead assets (books, CDs, etc.) into current assets on the likes of eBay
- Pre-test a larger entrepreneurial activity at lower risk
- And remember to save money on longer journeys using BlablaCar.

One exciting aspect of the gig economy is that concepts are evolving all the time. By the time you read this, some of the above marketplaces will have morphed into something new, or will have been replaced by a more relevant and productive service.

THRIFTY THINKING OVERHEAD-REDUCTION PROGRAMME

If you do the sums for five, ten or twenty years out, the relevance of Enlightened Thrift might suddenly come into focus. Even if you feel financially bulletproof, it could be that events over the coming years produce armour-piercing bullets, so the following list of suggestions might still be worth thinking about.

It is a somewhat random list, and some items will have more relevance to you than others:

- If possible pay off all debt, especially credit cards.
- If at all possible, pay off the mortgage, if you still have one. Interest is non-productive money, and the emotional high of paying it off is fantastic.
- If you have credit cards, pay them off in full monthly. Aim to use them only as a financial convenience, not as a very high-cost way of staying afloat.
- Remember that using credit cards to buy *things you don't need* is not in the game plan for Enlightened Thrift (and some might say is profoundly daft).
- If you are struggling with understanding finance, invest in books and courses to get a handle on how it works and what all the terms mean.
- Avoid money that is easy to borrow: it costs more. And probably too much.
- Ask the simple question: Do I really need it?
- Don't rely on getting lucky to sort things out. Life isn't like that.
- If it's slightly cold, put on a jersey rather than the central heating.
- When looking at investing in an asset, ask yourself: Is this a genuine asset, or is it a future liability masquerading as an asset? And if it is a financial asset, do I really understand it – emotionally as well as intellectually?
- Money doesn't buy security; the Four Autonomies Mindset is a far better bet. Use it.

- Do worthwhile work: it is a better bet for achieving a sense of security than well-paid work.
- Where and when possible, cycle or walk – it's cheaper and better for you than using the car.
- When buying tickets for theatres, be aware that they can be seen just as well from the gods as from the stalls.

Do think up some of your own ideas to add to the list.

REMEMBER YOUR NON-FINANCIAL ASSETS – YOU'LL NEED THEM

Enlightened Thrift is both bracing and life-enhancing. It's bracing because it's a bit like a physical workout. You're not pitting yourself against the miles on the road, or the lengths of the pool, or the weights on the exercise machines, but the challenge is not dissimilar. It's back to basics, it's a challenge – and testing yourself is fun.

The life-enhancing aspect kicks in when you have taken on the challenge, succeeded, and you feel good about yourself. But it's worth remembering your non-financial assets to help you embrace it fully. These are just a few:

- You have a positive mindset
- You have a brave heart
- You are learning and growing
- You have a loving heart
- You are generous with your time and your money
- You are enthusiastic
- You have friends and a family

- You have some great memories
- You are kind
- You have a sense of humour
- You control how you feel
- You control how you spend your time
- You now appreciate everything.

THE GOAL OF ENLIGHTENED THRIFT

The goal of Enlightened Thrift is quite simply to increase your chances of having sustained prosperity at a level that enables you to enjoy the final decades of your life.

The alternative – Enforced Thrift – is demeaning and uncomfortable.

The subsidiary goal of Enlightened Thrift is to reduce the dangers of financial obesity. Financial obesity keeps you closed to the world and slows you down.

And by eliminating obesity, Enlightened Thrift frees – and keeps free – the arteries of compassion.

Perhaps most important of all, it will give you the well-grounded basis from which to adopt the Four Autonomies Mindset to take that real second bite of the cherry.

THRIFT AND THE FUTURE OF THE HUMAN RACE

The biggest threat in the next few generations is going to come from extreme weather, rising sea levels and water scarcity. Without melodrama, we can predict that if left unchecked, global warming threatens us with extinction.

'Modern society is based on the notion of plenitude ...
of being able to add more and more physical stuff ...
To survive we have to shrink how much we want.'

– Professor Richard Sennett, sociologist and polymath

In the near future, hopefully thrift will become not just the preserve of the enlightened few but the behaviour pattern of the majority. The urgent and important need for thrift will be supercharged by the likelihood of the world population approaching ten billion or so by the end of the century.

The chance of science and technology coming to our rescue is probably delusional. While we might not be around to see the worst consequences of consumerism, we can certainly set a precedent as to how to mitigate them. So Enlightened Thrift is not just a device to cope with reducing disposable income in our later years, but a necessary way of living if we are to survive as a species.

GET YOUR MOUTH WATERING FOR YOUR
SECOND BITE OF THE CHERRY

Let's consolidate what you might have learned in this chapter:

1. A must-read if fear or anxiety sometimes stalks your waking and sleeping hours is *Feel the Fear and Do it Anyway* by Susan Jeffers. It has the subtitle 'How to turn your fear and indecision into confidence and action', and it delivers.

2. Make a list of the first three things you are going to cut out, or cut down on, to start on your journey to Enlightened Thrift.

3. As a starting point for decluttering, take a look at Graham Hill's TED talk on how to cut down on stuff: ted.com/talks/graham_hill_less_stuff_more_happiness

Ideas to further explore your approach to Enlightened Thrift:

1. Another good book on finances is *Happy Money* by Elizabeth Dunn and Michael Norton. Its advice on how to spend for greater happiness is backed by shedloads of psychological research, and confirms the fact that spending money on others gives a bigger happiness boost than spending it on yourself.

2. Read *The Life-Changing Magic of Tidying* by Marie Kondoo. It even got my family de-cluttering.

3. Talk to the Citizens Advice Bureau, or other free debt-counselling services, to get a fresh perspective on your financial situation.

CHAPTER FOUR
AUTONOMY ONE – EARNING

'Everybody complains about their aches and pains and all that, but my friends are either dead, or are still working.'

– Larry Wiseman, film-maker (aged eighty-four)

SEVEN INSIDIOUS EXCUSES FORCEFULLY REJECTED BY HIGHLY EFFECTIVE PEOPLE

EXCUSE NO.2

My scrawny redundancy money/skinny pension means I can't take risks at my stage of life.

Rubbish! Your thinnish money pot means that to be happy you've either got to change things so you have more financial wealth and/or more income. OR you have to learn how to take control and enjoy living on less. We've covered this second option. This chapter covers the first option.

When I was going through the traumas of the early-nineties recession I lost two stone in weight worrying about what was going to happen to the company, the employees, the suppliers, even the customers, who would lose a destination store for good advice on sports shoes.

When the situation finally resolved itself, and all were saved, I was still desolate. Everything I had worked for was gone, even if it was in capable hands. Apart from a short consultancy period with the new owners I was left with virtually nothing. And certainly no future source of income.

In the Western world, money is widely accepted as the sole criterion of wealth. The Industrial Revolution and the rise of capitalism in the nineteenth century set the pattern of equating wealth with money. Before that time the word was more widely interpreted as a concept. Indeed it was Karl Marx, living in London in the middle of the nineteenth century, who wrote 'money is becoming the universal, self-constituted value of all things. It is therefore robbing the whole world, human as well as natural, of its own individual values.' With their powerful nod towards the environmental challenges we now face, the words could almost have appeared in an article in the serious press today.

It is a deep irony that Russia, a country that espoused his teachings for almost a century, ended up demonstrating Marx's point with great clarity. Under the communist regime, the Soviet Union did not have financial wealth (although, arguably, deeply desired it) because the system didn't work very well. In fact, it had a very small and very inefficient economy.

What it did have was cultural and intellectual riches. It was still producing great writers, like Nabokov and Solzhenitsyn (though writing partly abroad). Its music and ballet continued to be world renowned, and it had a committed education system that produced some of the highest global literacy rates. The country also produced many engineers and scientists – even winning the race into space with Yuri Gagarin. It was good at both physical and intellectual sport (counting chess as a sport). So it had lots going for it, and lots to be proud of.

The crumbling of communism released a form of capitalism that was red in tooth and claw; the accumulation of money by fair means or foul – arguably at a level higher than most civilised countries – seemed to take over as the main definer of wealth. In Marx's words, money had again become 'the universal, self constituted value of all things'.

So as history and Marx tell us, wealth has many constituents, not only financial. And you, as a member of Generation Cherry, probably have many of these in more abundance than previous generations. Here are a few to consider:

- physical health
- mental health
- overall wellbeing
- physical ability
- education
- physical skills
- social skills
- ability to learn
- opportunity to learn
- peace of mind
- good relationships
- love
- freedom
- happiness
- choice
- self-respect

- friends
- family
- intellectual ability
- sense of humour
- good jokes to share
- kindness
- pets
- appreciation of nature
- good books
- meals with people you love.

It's not an exhaustive list, but take your pick. You're richer than you thought!

And don't forget your social capital. This too is an important part of your wealth. Your social capital is the value you can take from the network of friendships and positive relationships you have built up in all aspects of your life over the years.

Unlike some of today's younger workers, whose connections have been developed on digital social networks, your networks are less likely to be digital and more likely to be of the traditional physical kind. Trust – the key element of any business or personal relationship – is easier to build and is likely to last longer if you have looked someone in the eye, and built up mutual understanding and respect over a period of time.

But your social capital is not inert wealth. It needs nurturing and, like fruit, should not be allowed to wither on the vine. In the words of Dr Johnson, who compiled the first English Dictionary, friendships should be kept in a state of 'constant repair'.

Going back to the story of my personal voyage into the discovery of the meaning of true wealth ... After feeling sorry for myself for a bit, I decided to sit down and look for the positives in the situation.

There were many. I had a fantastically supportive wife, two lovely young children, a reasonable marketing brain, a healthy body, a wide spread of interests and a basic love of life and of people. So, apart from money, I was in great shape.

You may have noticed that the one thing I left out but that should be present on the list of wealth ingredients above is a positive outlook. It took me a long time to appreciate that the more positive your mindset, the more wealth elements there will be on your list, and the more you will appreciate the rich variety of your wealth. And the more you will relish, and benefit from, the autonomies.

Indeed, a positive attitude unlocks the treasure chest of your wealth.

EARNING: WHY WOULDN'T YOU?

So, on the important dimensions of human wealth you are hopefully in reasonable shape. On the narrow definition of financial wealth, however, you may or may not be. Given the uncertainties for all of us in terms of how long we might live, and our inevitably increasing vulnerability to mental and physical deterioration, our financial needs are uncertain.

If we are unlucky enough to have a stroke or some other disabling affliction, we might find ourselves in a care home. If so, the costs over an extended period will be significant. State funding is likely to diminish, or dry up altogether. Caught in the crossfire of a ballooning elderly population, and burgeoning healthcare costs as new, evermore expensive treatments become available, governments are unlikely to provide the cavalry to ride to our rescue. This means we, or our relatives, will have to cough up.

So income from working while we still can could come in handy. We may think we have things covered, but if we live another ten, twenty, thirty, forty years, our financial situation could change radically – for any number of reasons – over that length of time.

While also being aware of your life's riches and wealth, work will bring with it many broader riches beyond income. But to realise them and achieve true autonomy we still need to keep working on creating and sustaining sources of income.

While it might seem obvious, I think it's worth listing and reiterating a few of the benefits of a continuing financial income that people outside of the conventional workplace often overlook:

- It can be a lifesaver if you have a small redundancy pot, skinny pension or emaciated savings.
- You can give to worthwhile causes if you have a surplus.
- You can help out family members in need.
- Working keeps you in touch with the real world and how people are thinking and feeling.
- With money you have more chance of getting rapid medical assessments and solutions to health problems.
- Working gives you a chance to contribute, and be valued.
- You can put money into a Learning Pot to pay to develop new knowledge or skills (more about this later).
- Even if it's low paid, work gives you the chance to socialise, or to give back.

- Socialising and building new relationships can be crucial as friends and loved ones start to die, just when you need them most.
- Earning can build an extra nest egg for when financial sorrows come in battalions (which they usually do).

You could be feeling a bit smug about your financial situation. If you are, these benefits still provide a pretty powerful case for continuing to actively work. Even if it's only for one or two days a week.

And if you're not feeling financially smug, you could start to think about a different attitude to work. This is your second bite of the cherry, remember, so you have the opportunity to think hard about your true skills and interests before working out how they can best be employed at work. Above all, at work you enjoy.

WORKING ON. AND ON.

An HSBC global study showed that in the UK the number of people working on past the state pension age has doubled in the last twenty years to one and a half million. In other European countries the figures are far higher, and later life working is much more accepted as a normal part of life. And in both the US and the UK almost 20 per cent of people said they thought they would never be able to retire fully, as their savings or incomes were insufficient.

Unfortunately for women, more of you have to work on through necessity. The reasons are numerous. Historically, women have tended to work either in lower-skilled, lower-paid jobs or to lose out on promotion in more highly paid managerial jobs or through having time out for children. Also, many were paid less for doing the same jobs as men. Unconscionable – however, it still goes on.

For whatever reason, women's savings are less, and their ability to earn serious money in retirement is likely to be less. Indeed, one study indicated that women are three times more likely to be solely dependent on a state pension than men.

Going forward, when women rule the world of work (they have all the assets: higher educational attainments, better socialising skills, higher emotional intelligence, stronger multi-tasking skills) the balance is likely to change dramatically. But for now, most women will have to work harder to equalise their earning power with men. In the future, it might well be the other way round.

WORKING ON AND ON AND ENJOYING IT

I am talking about income from work, not necessarily a job as such. And that can be much more fun. You may love your job. That's great. Keep working at it – or something similar, where you can use existing skills. But in a world where jobs are disappearing and changing as a concept, it's probably better to think in terms of work.

What I'm suggesting is that before you go piling into what in the US is called an 'encore career' (i.e. a post-redundancy or conventional retirement age job), pause and have a think.

You may want to work in your existing area of expertise. Or where you can adapt your existing skills to new opportunities. You may want to look at a new area that excites you. Something you've always wanted to try. Something, even, that takes you right out of your comfort zone.

The point is this: not only do we have to rethink where we might work in the future, we also need to rethink how we might work. Because, whether we are aware of it or not, most of us have spent years working within the straitjacket that is a job. As Seth Godin, a profound thinker in this area, has pointed out, the carefully constructed CV is just proof of a history of compliance.

It's proof that you turn up on time, fulfil the requirements of your job specification, that you accept the wage offered, and you wait patiently for the next wage rise. Even if you rebel, and change jobs, or negotiate a higher wage, you are still a captive within the system. You have little or no autonomy. You are ticking boxes in a system controlled by fear, not passion or freewill.

Competence and compliance are fine, but we've done that, worn the T-shirt. Now we have the chance to be pioneering, and to design our own.

Enlightened business leaders strive for diversity in their organisations, not because they're good citizens and think they should, but because they know that homogeneity leads to conformity. Multiple studies show that what is required for a team to be productive is **creativity** and **adaptability**.

Creativity and adaptability are poisoned by conformity and compliance. If people all think the same, nothing fresh or original happens. Stasis doesn't produce growth. Entropy ensues. Ultimately, whole organisations die if they cannot innovate.

I am not advocating that everyone should change careers, or go through a kind of work mid-life crisis. If you enjoy what you do, that's great. Keep going. And if you want to have a change from stress and responsibility for a bit, and fancy stacking shelves in a supermarket, or working in a bar or a restaurant, that's fine too. As is taking a break from work to get your breath back.

What I am suggesting is that if you are up for it, this is a great opportunity to take a look at doing something different. Something you've always hankered to do, or something radical and a bit scary. Perhaps even something that's also worthwhile and socially valuable. And to do it in a way that gives you autonomy, control over the way earning fits into your life.

JOIN THE GIG ECONOMY

The impact on economic growth globally since the greed of the financiers caused the devastation of 2008 has been drawn out and painful. Economic growth is no longer a given, and income inequality is ugly, and getting uglier.

What's been called Ponzi Prosperity (Charles Ponzi is currently serving over a hundred years in a US prison for his massive pyramid selling fraud) has been replaced by prolonged austerity, as nations struggle to cope with, and hopefully reduce, the debt mountains fuelled by the lending spree that took place in the early years of the century.

And these less benign economic conditions have unfortunately polarised people's politics. Repeating history, the well-off with right-wing leanings are again rejoicing in austerity. It doesn't touch them, but it gives them the chance to cut further what they see as a bloated state. For them the state is not hospitals, schools and pensions, but spongers who use welfare services they have no way of paying for.

As most of the UK press is currently right wing, it has managed what would seem an almost impossible feat. It has persuaded voters that it is not the rich, who tend to avoid paying taxes, but the poor who are the social and economic vultures.

But inspiration comes from an unlikely source: our children. Because the bleak economy, with its high unemployment for young people, has had one unexpected benefit: It has got parents off the backs of their children who can't find conventional jobs. Parents can't pester and hector, because they know their child is not to blame for being unable to find a high-paying job for life.

Young people training for the professions (doctors, lawyers, etc.) are more or less exempt, because it's business as usual. They will get well-paid jobs, which may – for the time being, at least – come with pensions attached. Those going into finance, or corporate business, are likely to be OK, too.

But for most of the young, the current economic conditions are far from jolly, and work as a concept has become much more fluid. It's no different for Generation Cherry, so it would make sense to follow the young into the gig economy. Let's find out a bit more about what this entails.

SLASHERS IN THE GIG ECONOMY

Most of the younger generation aren't qualified for, or emotionally suited to, conventional jobs and careers, even if they were available. So they duck and dive, and bob and weave as freelancers. They may not call themselves freelancers, but that's what they are. They will be self-employed, although technically they may be employed for a few days a week as a teacher, or hospital worker.

They are creating – and taking advantage of – **the gig economy**. This is an increasingly important element of today's on-demand economy – enabled by the benefits of digital technology. More and more people – and especially young people – are working a variety of gigs, often across various types of work. It might be numerous gigs in a single line of activity – say copywriting or teaching – or they are doing one-off projects across a range of activities.

The ones doing gigs in several types of work are the **slashers**. Slashers derive their name from the / symbol, which differentiates different concepts in a more distinct and dramatic way than a semi-colon. They will have several sources of income – from photography/graphic design/supply teaching/sound recording/DJ-ing/composing/tutoring school children/care working/doing temporary work for their friends who have conventional jobs. And many more besides.

While this might initially sound chaotic and insecure, the amazing and joyous thing is that they are optimistic. And they have an optimism despite not having a fixed salary which would allow them to take paid holidays, or to plan economically for the future.

SELF-EMPLOYED PEOPLE IN GENERAL ARE HAPPY, BUT SELDOM RICH

This goes for freelancers and self-employed people across the piece. It's not just the young, who are naturally optimistic, but the majority are happy in this situation. After all, they have control over their own working lives – who they work for, and when and where.

The highly regarded Trajectory Global Foresight consultancy tracks satisfaction levels of workers with full-time jobs against those who are self-employed. While 35 per cent of full-time employees have a high level of satisfaction with their jobs, this rises to 45 per cent amongst the self-employed.

This increased level of happiness extends beyond their work – 46 per cent of those in full-time work claim to have a high satisfaction with their lives overall, but this rises to 52 per cent amongst the self-employed.

The killer figure is that while all studies show self-employed people tend overall to earn less than those with full-time jobs, their level of satisfaction with their earnings is higher. Of course hardly anyone is content with their level of earnings (as we've seen, most of us would like at least a little bit more), but 23 per cent of full-time employees say they have a 'high level of satisfaction with their finances'. Astonishingly, given that most of them are earning less, a higher percentage – 26 per cent – of self-employed workers claim a 'high level of satisfaction with their finances'. A UK study by the City & Guilds was more emphatic:

While 58 per cent of people in employment were happy (rather than having a high level of satisfaction) this shot up to 85 per cent amongst the self-employed.

ENTREPRENEURS ARE ALSO HAPPY, AND SOMETIMES RICH

The good news is that taking the first bite of the cherry of entrepreneurship is becoming more and more frequent for those of us of more mature years. We appreciate the risks involved more than the young, and can usually accommodate them better. This growth is partly down to numbers – our demographic is a large one and getting larger. And it's partly down to businesses being so much easier to set up today.

Technology means that many functions that would have been troublesome and costly to set up, like accounts or HR, can now be done yourself online or outsourced until scale means you can bring them back in.

Far more importantly, more mature people have more business – and life – experience. They have a better feeling for what might work. Not only that, they have a network of business colleagues and contacts, who can become advisors, helpers and possibly customers.

Financially, if necessary, they often have savings – or access to money. So older entrepreneurs have a lot going for them.

> More experienced entrepreneurs have inventiveness in their bloodstream. And they have more understanding of what problems need to be solved. Take the problem of needing two pairs of spectacles – one for long and one for short sight. This was solved by Benjamin Franklin, the polymath and serial inventor in the 1780s. And he was seventy-six – yes, seventy-six – years old when he cracked it, by inventing bi-focal lenses.

When considering becoming an entrepreneur it's important to understand that the stereotype of the undergraduate in his college room creating a new tech start-up is yesterday's news. Today's successful start-ups – even in technology – are generally founded by people of mature years.

A recent study by Duke University in the US of 549 successful technology start-ups showed that twice as many winners are over fifty than under twenty-five. Not only do the older entrepreneurs start more businesses, they start more successful ones – 70 per cent of the businesses lasted more than five years, compared to 28 per cent of younger entrepreneurs.

A study by Barclays Bank in the UK shows that new businesses started by the over fifties showed the lowest failure rates. And they now account for nearly a quarter of their new businesses. Even more positive was the finding that 95 per cent of the older entrepreneurs said they were happy with their decision to have a go.

THE OUTPUT AND THE GOAL: TO CREATE VALUE EVERY DAY

Whatever kind of work (or kinds of work, if you go plural) you decide to get involved in, your goal will be to do more than just turn up. Turning up on its own won't give you a second bite of the cherry. Turning up is stasis. A route to pipe-and-slippers old-style withdrawal from the world. Waiting for the final retirement from life when the need for any type of effort is terminally superfluous.

The key to finding work that is interesting, stimulating and possibly worthwhile is to think as an entrepreneur. That means thinking in terms of creating value. You might not see yourself as an entrepreneur, but if you think in terms of creating value, that's just what you are.

And creating value will make you feel excited. And will require you to be innovative and engaged. There will be dull bits – there always are. But the work will get your juices going.

Creating new value means bringing fresh energy to bear on your work every day. To inspire colleagues, customers, or clients with your enthusiasm. To create synergy, so people spark off you, and the result is bigger, better, more satisfying and more fun.

And with energy and enthusiasm, the value you create will be a broad church. New value can involve:

- Having fresh ideas yourself
- Stimulating others to have fresh ideas
- Bringing enthusiasm to a project that's running out of steam
- Spotting a trend that could help your team or organisation
- Providing resilience and positivity when under pressure
- Being the go-to person for challenging projects
- Providing humour and humanity in awkward situations
- Having integrity when people are tempted
- Having foresight – avoiding cock-ups.

You get the idea.

WHAT KIND OF WORK AND WHERE DO I FIND IT?

Work that absorbs you is no longer work. Time flies. You wonder where it has gone when you look at the clock, and you feel good about the space you are in and the way you have spent your time. Psychologists call this being in a flow situation. Awareness of your surroundings is turned down, and you are willingly and enjoyably submerged in the moment.

Your current work situation will obviously be particular to you. To move to having work rather than a job, to join the gig economy and think like an entrepreneur, the first step is to map out some basic decisions, based on questions such as:

- Is the work you are going to do or create full- or part-time?
- Is it in your existing area of expertise or experience?
- Is it something new and challenging?
- Does it just need the tailoring of your existing skill set?
- Will it require new learning or training?
- What level of income will you be looking for?

If you are going to continue in your current line of work – perhaps even stay in the same or a similar job – proceed directly to Go, and collect £200. Keep going, but do think about how you can find fresh methods of adding value.

If you are going to try something new, well done! Finding ways to create value in a new environment will be challenging, fun and comfort-zone enlarging.

Here are a few more questions to chew on:

- What areas of activity especially interest you?
- What issues or projects can you bring passion to?
- What do you need to learn in order to be able to offer new value?
- What experience do you need (if any) to be sure your new value is relevant?
- What resources can you tap into to make it happen?
- Why are you especially well equipped to supply it?

The essence of an entrepreneurial approach is to bring enthusiasm, energy and resilience to the party. But above all, you need insight. Insight is what identifies the problem or the opportunity, so that a solution – the new value – can be created.

The next chapter is all about Learning. Learning gives us perspective, insight and understanding. These are the building blocks for an entrepreneurial approach.

GET YOUR MOUTH WATERING FOR YOUR
SECOND BITE OF THE CHERRY

Let's consolidate what you might have learned in this chapter:

1. Draw up your Wealth Check. Identify all the aspects of Human Wealth you possess, including your social capital.

2. Start thinking about what work you might do, rather than what job you might take. And consider multiple work streams.

3. If you are going to stay in the same job, or line of work, think about how you might bring a more entrepreneurial approach to it.

Ideas to explore this element further:

1. Talk to some people who work for themselves, or are entrepreneurs, and get their take on work.

2. Have a few brainstorming sessions – on your own, or with friends – and come up with an idea or two that might be the genesis of a business.

3. Take advantage of the profusion of websites for freelancers. Explore Freelancer.com or Elance-oDesk.com. Fill out some forms. See how your skills and experience might supply answers to some of the demand in the marketplace.

CHAPTER FIVE
AUTONOMY TWO – LEARNING

'We called him Tortoise,
because he taught us.'

– Lewis Caroll

SEVEN INSIDIOUS EXCUSES FORCEFULLY REJECTED
BY HIGHLY EFFECTIVE PEOPLE

EXCUSE NO.3

At my age I have enough knowledge and experience to get by.

Such thinking reveals both ignorance and laziness. As a rule of thumb, the brighter and more knowledgeable a person is, the more they realise they have more, much more, to learn. And the more effort they put in, the more enjoyment they get out of learning. Only the profoundly idle will risk their knowledge shrinking (shrinking because knowledge around us is continually growing). Knowing just enough to get by won't win you a really juicy second bite of the cherry.

We are fortunate to live in an age when lifetime learning is not only a widely accepted concept, but one that is encouraged by tax breaks in several countries. The professional and business worlds understand that the rate of change in all areas demands that their managers and employees keep up to speed on what is going on in their sphere of operation.

Unfortunately, many learners in their more mature years see it as another example of compliance and box ticking, rather than as an opportunity to refresh skills and gather new insights.

The truth is that feeding the mind is like feeding the body. It should be done daily and continuously. With very little dieting. We are either learning and growing, or we are withering and dying.

THE TIME: 6 FEBRUARY 1958. THE PLACE: MUNICH AIRPORT.

The snow was swirling, sticking to the windscreen of the Airspeed Ambassador's cockpit. The crew looked anxiously at the dials. They'd just filled up at a refuelling stop in Munich on their way back from Belgrade, carrying a young and brilliantly talented Manchester United side that had just qualified for the semifinals of the European Cup.

The snow and ice on the runway had caused them to abort twice before getting near to lift-off speed. They decided on a third attempt, and went for it.

They accelerated, gathering speed at full throttle. They took off, and for a few moments it looked as if they would make it. But they never became fully airborne. The plane hit a fence, then a house, and finally broke in two.

Twenty-one of the crew and passengers died instantly, and two more died later. Eight of the dead were some of Manchester United's most gifted players.

One of the dead was Tommy Taylor. Tommy was seen as one of England's best ever centre forwards. Fast, strong and imperious in the air, he was called 'magnifico' by the Real Madrid legend Alfredo di Stéfano. Tommy was twenty-six, with a glittering future in football ahead of him.

The deaths of all those killed were tragic, but his death seemed particularly poignant. His sister-in-law, going through his effects, made a discovery that intensified the sadness of the loss of potential: 'We found two little black and yellow books. One was *Teach Yourself Public Speaking*, and the other was *Teach Yourself Maths*. It broke my heart when I saw those. They just showed how much he wanted to improve himself.'

Tommy Taylor, star of Manchester United and England, was still keen to learn and grow.

WHAT KIND OF LEARNING?

'The mind is not a vessel to be filled but a fire to be lighted'. This pithy aphorism, distilled from Plutarch's *On Listening to Lectures* some two thousand years ago, like all true wisdom is timeless.

Learning is thus a stimulus. It lights the fire. It's what will keep you plugged into the world around you. It broadens your identity, gives you more things to wax lyrical about. And it ensures you are better able to add value (i.e. contribute more).

This isn't cloud cuckoo land. If you are developing yourself so you can really enjoy and benefit from a second wind, you will want to get a bang out of what you do – and that comes from a passion to learn, the passion learning gives you and the consequent extra value you'll be able to add all round.

I'm not suggesting you parade either your knowledge or your new insights to all and sundry, but it's very easy to spot someone fired up by life and learning. And it's infectious – colleagues, friends and family will sense you're at least as bright and sharp as they are in spite of the fact that you might be ten or forty years their senior. Learning doesn't stop and it's inspiring to see people who embrace that mindset – inspiring because they've taken control of how they use their time and chosen to stoke their fires.

There are many kinds of learning. Most are relevant to increasing the sweetness of the second bite of our cherry, but some are more valuable than others.

More than ever, we are looking for *insight* rather than *facts*. *Understanding* rather than *knowledge*. Don't get me wrong, knowledge is important. Both for keeping up to date with your existing area of expertise, if you wish to carry on with that, or learning about new areas that interest you. But more important is to be constantly evaluating the knowledge you are taking in. Not just for its veracity and level of interest, but for the insights you can draw from it that might fit into other areas of your life. The most unexpected things can end up being relevant.

Unstructured though it may be, we are incredibly lucky to live in an age of such widespread online information. At the click of a mouse we have access to a wealth of knowledge and insight.

Take an example. **TED lectures** are a feast to savour. Great thinkers and doers share their knowledge and wisdom in extremely digestible portions. For a taster, I'd highly recommend taking a look at one of Dan Pink's lectures on motivation: ted.com/talks/dan_pink_on_motivation

In it he makes afresh the distinction between intrinsic motivation – the things that get your personal motivational juices flowing – and external motivation – the carrots and sticks that influence you from outside. And he demonstrates the surprising truth that incentives in many situations can be *counterproductive*. Carrots can make people less incentivised, so they put in less effort. All in all, Dan's lecture gives a useful insight into human behaviour.

This talk is interesting. It is also pertinent for some of the thinking in this book. But crucially it confirms that learning is not just about information or knowledge but about insight. Insights stumbled upon when you make time to learn, such as Dan Pink's, can impact on both how you think, feel and act, and how you influence others to think, feel and act. They can cross-fertilise your other autonomies. And ultimately bring infectious enthusiasm and add value across the board.

LEARNING WHAT THE HELL YOU WANT TO DO

All this is supercharged when you find meaning in what you do, if it chimes with your purpose in life. But what is your purpose?

If you want to keep working at what you already do, or you have a burning passion to do something you have wanted to do all your life – skip this bit.

For the rest of us, finding our purpose is a tricky thing. If you don't have a strong desire to carve wooden objects, or to sail singlehandedly around the world, it's daft to pretend you do.

But spending time trying to figure it out, even if it takes you down some dead ends, is part of learning. The journey will teach you things. I've written extensively on finding your purpose (see my book *How to Make a Difference* and the website howtomakeadifference.co.uk, which includes a workbook). And while I've written on it, and thought about it, I still haven't found something I would say I am totally *passionate* about. It's simply not easy.

I have identified lots of things I love doing, and I am confident that Abraham Mazlow's highest level of motivation – finding fulfilment through helping others find fulfilment – was written for me, but the exact medium I need to achieve that is still fairly fluid. I'm now comfortable with that, knowing I'm still looking and learning along the way.

One thing to note is that *fulfilment* is the goal, rather than *happiness*. Happiness often accompanies fulfilment, but not always, and sometimes only arrives further down the line.

Fulfilment is active and profound. It comes from intellectual and emotional satisfaction and engagement. Happiness tends to be a mood that reflects external events, though it can be self-engendered. It can also be fleeting. Fulfilment, on the other hand, is the result of finding meaning and satisfaction by striving to find or achieve one's purpose.

So thinking about your purpose is important, but not that easy. Making the decision to start the journey is the crucial, brave first step, and learning as you go is all part of the learning autonomy mindset.

We'll explore courage and your purpose in more detail later in the book. The rest of this chapter will look at practical ways to implement continuous and continued learning.

MAKING TIME TO LEARN – WISDOM WEDNESDAYS

It's easy to get out of the practice of learning. As we get older, we tend to value our non-working time highly, and see it as a reward. A time for a passive enjoyment, nothing too taxing, thank you very much.

Downtime for the brain can be very resuscitating if you are in a highly stressed environment. But having left the stress of working full-time for other people in a non-autonomous environment, putting your brain in neutral would be regarded as old-fashioned unemployment or retirement by another name. Remember, by being active and engaged we are getting a second bite of the cherry. That means we are excited by the opportunity and are willing to put in some effort, enthusiasm and commitment. Ironically, you'll probably find the effort enjoyable, so it won't seem like work at all.

What I recommend is putting aside a set time each week. I call it Wisdom Wednesday.

I commit to watching instructive videos (like TED), or reading an uplifting book or essay at the same time each week for between one and two hours – more if possible. In one go, so I can concentrate. I also take any scrap of time I can for more lecture watching, listening to podcasts (especially when running – it takes your mind off the discomfort) or reading books or magazines.

However much I enjoy what I am absorbing, I also try to be actively engaged with the speaker or author, evaluating as I go, looking for insight. And where appropriate, I take notes, which I revisit at least once or twice so the spaced repetition can better fix them in my brain.

While Wisdom Wednesday – or Thought-Provoking Thursday – a fixed chunk of time – is important, it's also worth plugging into some lighter daily fare. There are several blogs that are worth following, but one I would highly recommend is Seth Godin: sethgodin.typepad.com

Seth's daily taster is often pretty nourishing. They're usually short, challenging, interesting and enjoyable. And worth pondering.

BUILD A PERSONAL LEARNING POT READY FOR DEPLOYMENT

Whatever your age, or stage in your working life, it is worth putting a little money aside for learning. This may be for retraining in the sense of updating existing knowledge and skills, or for learning something entirely fresh. Going to a conference on an area of interest can be especially stimulating. As well as learning from the speakers, interacting with the other delegates can be a rich source of enlightenment.

Government cutbacks around the world mean that you can no longer rely on state-supplied systems of education and training for citizens of any age. Be ready with a fund you can spend on creating new, more focused skills and knowledge.

DON'T FEEL GUILTY ABOUT SPENDING TIME LEARNING

Life, of course, gets in the way, so you are unlikely to find it convenient to put aside the same time slot every week. The crucial thing is to avoid it slipping down the priority list, and not to feel guilty investing time in it.

If you are watching a TED lecture, or reading *The Economist*, and someone comes into the room, it's very tempting to feel guilty about what you are doing. It doesn't seem like work. There's lots of stuff to shovel, and you are patently not shovelling it.

Resist the temptation to quickly get on with something more obviously useful or productive. *It's your learning and thinking time – protect it, and feel proud you are keeping fresh and engaged intellectually.*

It's easier said than done, but remember, the whole point of autonomy is that *you* are in control. If you decide you will put aside a slug of time each week to develop yourself – so you can be better at what you do, and enjoy it more – that's your privilege to enjoy. Feel good about it, and ignore the snidey snipers who want to bring you down to their level of intellectual and emotional sclerosis.

ENFORCED SELF-RELIANCE MEANS LEARNING IS CRUCIAL

As I touched on in the previous chapter, given the way the labour market is evolving, it's probably worth thinking in terms of creating income-generating *work*, rather than a job. Jobs are likely to become a dated concept as portfolio workers have multiple income streams from multiple projects or initiatives.

As the on-demand economy develops, the predictions are that what the business experts call contingent workers – and what you or I would call independent contractors, temporary contract, or freelance workers – will take on chunks of work on the outside that historically were carried out by employees on the inside.

As these chunks are parcelled up and outsourced, the impact within organisations will inevitably put pressure on internal employees to develop their skills in order to avoid becoming redundant. And because employers will find it inefficient to pay for so much training when they can get the benefits more cheaply from already trained freelancers, employees will increasingly have to fund their training themselves.

So whether you are thinking about freelancing, or staying within a conventional organisation, in the words of *The Economist* magazine: 'People will have to master multiple skills if they are to survive in such a world – and keep those skills up to date. Professional sorts in big service firms will have to take more responsibility for educating themselves.'

So continuous learning – often self-prescribed – is becoming crucial to surviving in the job market for young people as well as older people. As most jobs in general morph into work, the security that used to go with jobs as a concept will decline further.

The benefit of the flexibility that comes with work rather than a job is potentially great for older people, as it opens up all sorts of opportunities. But the lack of security implicit in the deal could prove challenging for our children and grandchildren. The lack of ancillary benefits – such as healthcare, continuous training and personal development – means self-reliance is, and will be, the name of the game. What is in effect the re-casualisation of work is, in a sense, taking us back to the times before the Industrial Revolution, when all labour was casual.

The upside is that whereas most casual labourers at that time worked on farms for little pay, at least today the work will largely be in the Knowledge Economy (i.e. digital, technical, creative, etc.) and service industries (healthcare, law, teaching and so on), where it is likely to be a whole lot more interesting, less physically demanding and, sometimes, more highly rewarded.

One further upside is that women will not be penalised so much for having children. If careers become a legacy concept of the Job

Era, there will be no need for career breaks. Women will be able to work freelance in the gig economy as and when it suits them during childcare periods, while spending other pockets of time learning new skills and insights. They are also likely to get a whole lot more support from partners, who will also be freelancing, and thus more flexible with their working time.

Part of the Autonomy Mindset is taking responsibility for your own learning. This is a privilege – because you decide what and how much you are going to learn.

But it can also be a whole lot of fun. There are no set books. And seemingly random bits of learning can feed into new ideas and fresh insights. Learning becomes almost childlike again. You are like a child in a kindergarten. It's all new. It's all exciting. It's an adventure. And if imaginatively directed, will lead on to fortune.

CROSS-POLLINATE WITH OTHERS TO SEED NEW IDEAS

Fresh inputs and a broad view can be incredibly helpful in learning, especially if they are stimulated by curiosity and passion. Sharing curiosity and passion by putting together what the personal development books (highly recommended, by the way, for Second Biters) call a **Mastermind Group**, is a great way to supercharge this. A Mastermind Group is one of the most effective ways to learn, as well as to create value.

You form a group of four to ten people who are keen to find stimulus from discussing ideas and thinking about new, interesting or relevant ways to provide benefits where none existed before, or address problems that need overcoming. The group can be virtual, online or better still, in person. The group should be as diverse in make-up as you can make it, so that differing backgrounds can spark off each other. Different perspectives lead to fresh insights, and fresh ideas.

What have chicken farming and premature babies got in common? Not natural bedfellows you might say. And what have hunting with guns and dogs got to do with Velcro?

Cross-fertilisation of ideas and/or inspired connections of facts often have felicitous outcomes. It's the opposite of linear thinking and it stems from either diversity of contributors and their backgrounds, or from one inspired person spotting connections no one had perceived before.

Here are two examples, one French, one Swiss. Stéphane Tarnier was an obstetrician practising in Paris in the latter part of the nineteenth century. He was particularly interested in the survival of premature infants. Inspired by a device used by farmers to incubate chickens, he introduced a prototype device for babies into his Paris hospital in 1881. Using what he called his *couveuse*, or baby-warming device, he reduced infant mortality by 28 per cent. Thus the incubator was born.

George de Mestral was a Swiss civil engineer, who after hunting trips in the 1940s was faced with the perpetual problem of picking the burdock burrs off his legs, and his dog. A painstaking and infuriatingly slow process, as anyone who has had to do it will testify. Curious as to what made them so tenacious, he examined them under a microscope. He saw that they had hundreds of hooks that caught onto any loops that came into contact with them. It took him years to replicate the process and develop its application for clothing, but he eventually managed it. In 1955 he successfully patented the concept of Velcro.

The group should link up regularly – once a fortnight or once a month – and brainstorm and develop ideas that could lead to new businesses, social enterprises or fundable projects. Such a group has the benefit of not only creating and developing ideas, but also of having access to lots of other areas of learning and expertise (and possibly funding) through friends and contacts. They obviously bring the benefit of human interaction too.

If you live in a remote area and want to meet in person rather than online, then having only three, or even two, people in the group can work. Simply talking and exchanging ideas keeps your business mind active. It's just more effective with the critical mass and diversity of a slightly larger group.

Mastermind groups can be informal – created by you from worthwhile and plugged-in people you know or have met – or they can be more commercially organised. The latter are worth checking out (there are plenty on the internet to choose from), and they often have the added benefit of organising lectures or conferences that you can attend online or in person.

These lectures and conferences can become learning opportunities in their own right, and the socialising afterwards can be enjoyable and productive.

FIND A MUSE OR TWO

Theodore Zeldin, the glorious polymath and author of *The Future of Work* (do look him up online), suggests all of us should find a muse or two. This is a more personal and intimate version of the Mastermind Group.

Your muse can be anyone who stimulates you intellectually. They can be mentors or people you yourself mentor. I have several muses. They tend not necessarily to be close friends. They are people I enjoy meeting and spending time with – on the phone or in person – and who always spark ideas, and lead me to look at things in new ways. I always come away from talking to them with new insights and fresh perspectives.

Time spent with them is highly stimulating and highly productive. And, because there is no agenda involved, it is somehow less stressful than a Mastermind Group.

NETWORKING TO FIND NEW VALUE

This is a chewy one. Many people advise active networking as the source of inspiration when you are trying to create new value, or even just to find new sources of income.

I personally find active networking a pain. And it's even more painful if you are *being* networked. It feels like you are being grilled before being invited to join a cult.

A couple of years ago, I met an inspirational guy called Sasha Dichter, who is the chief innovation officer for Acumen. Acumen is a brilliant organisation that is finding new and effective ways to address poverty around the world. Take a look at acumen.org (and sign up to his blog).

A delightful and very bright individual, one of whose jobs is to raise money for the fund, he spoke at some length about the task of raising money for charity. His message was simple: *you are not asking for money, you are building a relationship.*

Networking, like fundraising, is not about selling yourself and having a thoroughly unenjoyable and ineffectual experience in the process. *It's about building a relationship* and genuinely learning about the other person.

It's much more interesting to listen, to ask questions and find out things about new people than worry about whether there is benefit in the conversation for you. It's about *learning from others.* Learning in the sense you are talking to someone with a view to finding out not only new information and ideas, but also if you can help them in some way. This means you are retaining your autonomy. You are in control because you are not disingenuously touting for business. You are genuinely seeking to learn, and to find out if you can bring benefit to the person you are talking to.

So, networking is about having an enjoyable conversation that may or may not bear fruit at some future date.

SELF-PAID SABBATICALS OR WORK PLACEMENTS

We touched on finding your purpose earlier. It's not easy but finding it sure makes life easier, more enjoyable and more fruitful. One possible route to finding your future niche is what I call self-funded sabbaticals or work placements of a week or so.

The idea is this: if you are still not totally confident of your purpose and future direction of work, suck one or two and see.

You know how you start a job and within a relatively short period of time you get that heart-in-the-boots feeling that *this is a mistake*. My first was such a job.

In the sixties, when I left university, jobs were everywhere. Nothing to worry about. But like many graduates, I didn't have a clue as to what I wanted to do.

My father, bless him, came to the rescue. A friend of his ran a medium-sized insurance company. They had introduced a graduate trainee scheme that fast-tracked entrants to exciting places, and gave them exciting challenges.

By the time I was offered the job, I had in fact applied to other companies, one in a very lively merchant bank. After discussion with my parents, I took the promising job in the insurance company.

It was unspeakable.

Not only did the graduate trainee scheme not exist, they had no intention of introducing one. The pace of work was glacial. They would give me what was intended to be a couple of days' work, and I would complete it within the hour. The people in my department literally spent most of the afternoon asleep. Indeed one woman eschewed coffee after lunch and had drinking chocolate instead, because coffee kept her awake.

At 4.45 in the afternoon there was a general movement, as the staff casually sauntered to the coat racks, and brought back their coats and hid them under their desks. At 5 p.m. there was a stampede for the door. It was the only time of the day when the staff moved at any speed above that of a snail.

In those days, stickability was a highly prized virtue. My parents had instilled in me that I had to stick any job for at least six months or I would be branded a fly-by-night, a ne'er-do-well. And in the culture of those times, they were probably right. I stuck it out more for my parents' sake than for any other reason, but six months later, I was off. Into another cul-de-sac, which this time lasted eighteen months.

I stayed eighteen months because although I knew it wasn't for me, I understood that the experience was beneficial. I was learning from experts in their business. Like selling and PR. Valuable experience, but not ultimately for me.

The point is that nowadays young people wouldn't stick it out for more than a few days. And they'd be right not to. And the further benefit of our culture today is that work experience is a recognised concept, as are sabbaticals. Both allow people to explore what excites them, what they are good at and what they feel at home doing.

You may need to do a bit of selling to the providers of the type of work you are exploring, but you have two great advantages. You are experienced and wise. And you are offering your considerable services for free.

Since writing this, I learn that Hollywood – and Robert De Niro – have made this idea into a film. Whether this validates the concept or not, I'm not sure, but it does indicate it has mileage!

LEARNING TO MASTER MASTERY

Finally, for this chapter, I will touch on mastery. Learning skills and areas of specialist knowledge can sometimes lead to mastery. It has a long and distinguished pedigree.

In the Middle Ages and beyond, apprentices in their tightly controlled guilds would work for years at learning their trade before being examined for the final recognition of becoming a master. They submitted what was called their *masterpiece* to be examined by other masters to see if they had reached the required level of expertise to be called a master in their own right.

Nowadays, being recognised as being a master is a bit more complex, but Nobel Prizes come pretty close to the old guild system of recognition. It is highly unlikely you will need to reach such a level in your chosen area of knowledge or expertise, but striving for it is becoming a hot topic in terms of work and employment.

If you have had a chance to look at some of Dan Pink's talks on work, life satisfaction and fulfilment, you will have seen that mastery is up there with autonomy as a key element.

In terms of business and commerce, it pops up frequently in management theory and people development. A great champion of it is Lynda Gratton, professor of management practice at the London Business School. Gratton recently undertook a wide-ranging and fascinating study on the future of work in the twenty-first century.

The study came to several enlightened and sensible conclusions. One of these was that non-specialist skills will be replaced by either technology or lower-paid alternatives in other parts of the world. Which makes sense. So, in-depth mastery will replace generalist skills, something to consider if you want to be indispensable and stay in work.

And because things change so rapidly in business, as in the wider world, there will be a further need for what she calls *serial mastery*. This means staying ahead of the curve, while recognising you need to be adaptable in terms of the evolving skills and knowledge of your sector as things develop.

I find myself nodding to this as it makes eminent sense. I then ask myself the question, 'OK, Tim, what are your specialist skills?'

And I wait for an answer. The longer I think about it, the less of an answer I have.

This leads to a choice of conclusions. Either I have been very lucky to have got away with it for so many years (which I have – see Imposter Syndrome, Chapter 1). Or I may have some generalist skills that I can focus on specific issues for short periods. Or I know how to find specialist skills, either through my network of friends and associates, or their network of friends and associates.

Either way, I have the ability to marshal specialist skills or knowledge, which means I can still bring some level of unique value to business or social enterprise.

So, my conclusion is that if there is any area where you can achieve mastery – go for it, big time. But if there doesn't seem to be one, define mastery in a more generous and relevant way when you come to think about what specialist skills you bring to the party. Mix it up with your networking. That wonderfully random person you met last week might be just the master you need one day.

THE JOY OF LEARNING

So, learning is our second major autonomy. It's about taking responsibility for our minds and firing up an eagerness for knowledge. It acknowledges that without making that effort, we'll start shrivelling (and our cherry will too). And that not only is it important to keep seeking out knowledge but that reflecting on it for insight is crucial.

It will give you the opportunity to discover, to unearth *what you need to know to equip yourself to create value* in your chosen new work.

It's about having an open and curious mind. Once you rediscover your youthful enthusiasm for knowledge, you'll love hoovering up new information and new ways of looking at things. Sharing it with others is also a joy – forwarding links to blogs or talks to colleagues, friends, or even your children and grandchildren.

It is not only uplifting, it will make the experience you have built up over the years so much more relevant.

It will update it, and plug it into a modern context of work.

All this means we become relevant, energised, alive. We grow. We have more to offer and will inevitably create more value as a result.

GET YOUR MOUTH WATERING FOR YOUR
SECOND BITE OF THE CHERRY

Let's consolidate what you might have learned in this chapter:

1. Build your Learning Pot – funds for books, courses, conferences on your area of interest. If it transpires you don't need it, spend it, and enjoy it as a windfall.

2. Wisdom Wednesdays: set aside a *specific* time each and every week for active learning. Don't be surprised if it becomes one of the most enjoyable parts of the week.

3. Start thinking now how you will create value today. And what learning you need to undertake to deliver it. And keep thinking.

Ideas to explore this element further:

1. Read *Strengths Finder 2.0* by Tom Rath to get a second opinion on your top five strengths. It's based on shedloads of data examining human strengths collected over the years by the Gallup company.

2. Keep a pad and pen by the bed to write down any ideas that occur to you in the night.

3. For further inspiration on learning, and the proof that it is never too late, look at the profoundly moving and motivational DO Lecture, by Dennis McIntosh (Do Australia, 2015): thedolectures. com/dennis-mcintosh-train-your-brain-like-a-muscle

CHAPTER SIX
AUTONOMY THREE – GIVING

'The character of a man can be gauged by his dealings with people who cannot possibly do him any favours.'

– Goethe

SEVEN INSIDIOUS EXCUSES FORCEFULLY REJECTED
BY HIGHLY EFFECTIVE PEOPLE

EXCUSE NO.4

I've been giving at work for decades. Give, give, give. I deserve a bit of payback now.

You may feel a need to receive some of the rewards from all your hard work, and to recover from not being properly recognised for your efforts, but forget it. This is a new start. You are in control, and you'll find you gain more on a personal level from giving than you could have thought possible.

Giving is empowering. You are in control because, quite simply, you are choosing to do the giving.

And whether it be your time, money or your ear, as Goethe says, you should not expect a reward. It has to be done wholeheartedly, without thought of reward. Seneca, the Roman philosopher who we saw promoting thrift in an earlier chapter, talks of the fact that **'there is no grace in a benefit that sticks to the fingers'**.

The mechanics of giving can be delicate and nuanced (see *The Gift*, the brilliant book by Lewis Hyde), but the essence of it is that the moment you even look for a positive reaction, let alone any sort of reciprocity or reward, the magic of giving dissolves.

But it's worth recognising that we also give because it makes us feel good. It gives great satisfaction to both the receiver *and the giver*. There is lots of evidence to prove it. And the autonomy – knowing we've made the choice to do the giving – is just part of the reward.

THE BENEFITS OF GIVING

Research reveals some pretty major pluses for helping others:

- **We feel good about ourselves**. Not only do we get mental satisfaction from giving, psychologists have identified a 'helper's high' – a warm glow that comes from the release of endorphins because you are both energised and calm at the same time.

- A study by Cornell University found that volunteering not only **increases your energy**, but also **your sense of mastery over life, and thus your self-esteem**.

- Other studies have shown that such positive feelings can even **strengthen and enhance the immune system**. They increase the body's number of T-cells – the cells in the immune system that help the body resist disease and recover quickly when you are ill.

- Generosity of time and heart means you **live longer** – and you are **healthier over that longer lifespan**. A study of nearly three thousand participants over an almost ten-year period, after controlling for age, health etc., found volunteers had death rates dramatically lower than those who didn't volunteer.

- **You can even lose weight**. A study of 615 Community Service Volunteers in the UK revealed that volunteers not only enjoy better mental health, and less sick days, but also noticeable weight loss.

- Interestingly, **older people who volunteer show greater health benefits than younger volunteers**. The reason for this, claim researchers who explored the data, is that older people undertaking volunteer activities are more likely to be provided with a **sense of purpose**. They feel they are performing a useful social role.

- Volunteering can improve **connection with community**. Researchers found that the social ties built up during volunteering can ward off a sense of isolation during difficult times.

- Perhaps most importantly, the experience of helping others leads to **a sense of greater self-worth and trust**.

- Giving often brings with it **new experiences**, which can also extend your comfort zone.

- You can potentially **learn new skills**, as you find out how to start a new charity, or put up shelves.

The proviso stipulated in one of the studies was that a 'volunteering threshold' needed to be met to reap the rewards of these benefits. The reassuring news is that the amount of time defined as the threshold was only one to two hours a week.

And then, of course, there are the beneficial impacts for those who receive the gifts of time and caring. Take just two:

- **It contributes to building social cohesion**. Most types of giving are social in nature. Whether it is a volunteering for a local charity, supporting a relative or friend in need of physical or emotional support, or donating time and/or money to a good cause, it is helping society to function better. By helping other people we are finding a common cause, which as well as helping individuals, binds us together.

- **It helps to avoid isolation**. This is the individual, human side of social cohesion. Generally, the people receiving the giving are isolated and vulnerable. It could be someone receiving debt counselling, a depressed person close to suicide, an addict, a homeless person, a prisoner frightened and desperate, an ex-service person suffering from post-traumatic stress, or an infirm elderly person without support trying to stay in their own home. The list is depressingly long, and dauntingly incomplete, and they all feel anxious, frightened and alone. Volunteering, whether directly or indirectly, to tackle this has a positive impact on reducing isolation.

So the opportunity to do good is almost infinite.

Before we move on, let's double underline it by rehearsing once more the magnitude and multiplicity of the benefits of being generous with one's time and one's self:

- We feel good about ourselves
- We have more energy
- We have a higher sense of self-worth
- We have an enhanced immune system
- We live longer, and are healthier over the increased lifespan
- We can lose weight
- Our trust level is higher
- We have a greater connection with our community
- We have a sense of mastery over our life.

It really is a no-brainer. But what, deep down, makes it so rewarding?

BEYOND THE BENEFITS: TRANSCENDENCE

'How selfish soever man may be supposed, there are evidently some principles in his nature which interest him in the fortunes of others, and render their happiness necessary to him, though he derives nothing from it, except the pleasure of seeing it… The greatest ruffian, the most hardened violator of the laws of society, is not altogether without it.'

– Adam Smith, The Theory of Moral Sentiments

The famous hierarchy of needs that Abraham Maslow outlined seems to me to be built on sound sense as well as sound psychology. His original hierarchy, of 1943, had five levels.

The first level is the need to satisfy basic physiological needs – breathing, food, sleep, excretion, etc. The second moves on to safety – protecting one's body, one's family etc. Once these basic needs are satisfied you can move up to the third level, which is love, friendship and belonging. The fourth step is esteem – respect from others, self-worth, etc.

Once this has been achieved, you can move to the highest level, which is termed Self-Actualisation. This is about seeking personal growth and peak experiences, self-fulfilment, reaching one's potential as a human being.

Over subsequent years, Maslow refined his model of human motivation, and ended up with a new top level, above Self-Actualisation. This level is the level of Transcendence.

Transcendence is reached by *helping others to achieve self-actualisation*. The essence of this has recently been confirmed by neuroscience research, but it always had the ring of truth.

So our highest motivator as human beings is to help other people. And not just to help them, but to help them find their fulfilment, and in so doing, find our own.

Some would say it's a high goal to aim for. I would argue that impact and effectiveness are, for most of us, more important than scale. Let's face it – not many of us have the ability, or the opportunity, to be Gandhi and transform the life chances of a nation. We can, however, potentially make a big impact on a more modest but still hugely worthwhile local or even one-to-one level.

A special-needs teacher can transform the abilities and chances of a child located somewhere on the autism spectrum. An elderly but active person can transform both the quality of life, and indeed life expectancy, of immobile and lonely neighbours. A volunteer with the Citizens Advice Bureau can positively affect the ability to cope, the self-worth, and the life chances of whole families by providing counsel that helps them reduce debt and get the show back on the road.

Parents, grandparents and those in close contact with the youngest generations – have a huge opportunity to approach transcendence. It may not feel like it at the time – bringing up children can be challenging and exhausting – but they have the privilege of being in a position to light the fire of learning in their children.

In a world where exam results and qualifications have tended to take over from delight in creativity, the arts and the humanities, there is work to do. And parents and grandparents are possibly the best positioned to undertake it.

Stoking the fire of their children and grandchildren's imaginations, their interest in solving problems, and the delight in fresh knowledge for its own sake, is a potentially transformative gift.

Transcendence can be achieved in taking a child from being an unwilling and possibly resentful fact-acquirer to an excited and motivated adventurer in the land of knowledge and insight. It can light their creative fires so they develop a hunger for learning for its own sake in areas they find exciting. It goes back to the root of the word education – the Latin words *ex ducere* – to bring out, lead forth, develop interests and talents that lie within someone.

So on a limited, personal level, we can all achieve intimations, or even manifestations, of Maslow's highest level of motivation.

Each one of us can achieve Transcendence: Self-Actualisation by helping others fulfil more of their potential.

OUR DESIRE TO GIVE BACK CAN BE SUPERCHARGED BY OUR GENERATIONAL OBLIGATION

As members of Generation Cherry we have a special obligation to give back.

The tough fact is that, owing to little fault of our own, **most of us now belong to a generation of takers rather than givers.** I suppose I am typical of many of my generation in that I had the many privileges outlined in the Introduction – free education through to graduate level and beyond; being able to buy my own house; work pensions; increases in the value of the property I own, etc.

But our children's generation doesn't look as though it will be so lucky. The economic outlook globally appears at best uninspiring. Economic performance by country will vary significantly, and growth looks set to be muted at best. Add to that the demographic shift in the developed world towards ageing, dependent populations and today's young will have to work a lot harder for a lot longer to get anywhere near enjoying what we have enjoyed.

Any sense of entitlement will need to be changed to one of gratitude. We've been very lucky, but we shouldn't rub it in by expecting more. The loss of skilled jobs, and the hollowing out of the middle class – all results of widening social inequality – will mean we'll need to help others as well as ourselves.

So reversing the narrative from taking to giving becomes almost a social imperative, as well as something desirable in its own right. Fortunately, as Maslow pointed out, we are all hardwired to try to reach the higher levels of motivation, and become givers.

There are endless ways to give. I've split the opportunities on offer to be socially useful and give back into five categories to help you consider what suits you best.

1. GIVING BY VOLUNTEERING

Kurt Hahn came from a wealthy Jewish family in Germany, where he founded the Salem School, which was one of the pioneers of experiential learning. The school used adventure education in the outdoors to develop character, independence of mind and resilience.

Forced to flee the Nazis in 1933, he came to England, where he co-founded Gordonstoun, a private school that further developed these ideas. He went on to found Outward Bound (1941), The Duke of Edinburgh's Award scheme (1956) and the Atlantic College (1962), which, along with academic achievement, has student participation in community service at its core.

As a pioneering educator who left a prodigious legacy of developing rounded, self-reliant individuals, his insight into motivation of the young was simple:

'There are three ways to win the young. You can preach at them – that is a hook without a worm.

'You can say: "You must volunteer." That is of the devil.

'And you can tell them "You are needed": That approach hardly ever fails.'

By and large, most of the readers of this book, like the writer, are privileged people living in a society that has too many underprivileged people in it. And one small way to correct this imbalance is to volunteer to help in a worthwhile social enterprise. The UK has one of the highest levels of volunteering for any Western country. So it's not a revolutionary suggestion.

Kurt Hahn's quote is timeless; it rings as true today as it did last century. But it doesn't only apply to the young – the same can be said for all age groups.

'One volunteer is worth ten pressed men', a saying that dates back to the days when the British Navy had to send out gangs to kidnap men to serve on its ships, demonstrates the hook without the worm. It was not surprising that those captured men, who dearly wanted to be at home and not forced on board a ship, were none too enthusiastic about their duties.

But being pressured into volunteering through some sense of guilt or feeling that you *should* – the 'must' from Hahn's quote – well, that can certainly 'be the devil'. While the scope of volunteering is enormous (mentoring and activism come under this too), across all its manifestations the quality of the results (for both giver and receiver) has one common characteristic: the energy of the volunteer.

If you are chivvied along and aren't there in both mind as well as body, you'll lack any kind of visible enthusiasm – and that missing energy will be more than apparent to your fellow volunteers. And your positive impact will be far lower than someone raring to go and give. In fact, from an organisation's or charity's point of view, a half-hearted volunteer can sometimes be *worse* than the devil – if positions are limited, someone doing less than their all is a nightmare.

Volunteering is still an incredibly important option in the Giving autonomy. But the manner in which you come to it greatly affects the efficacy. To hit the jackpot of giving 'that hardly ever fails', we need to feel needed – so we *want* to be there.

Unlike someone who is on the payroll to do a particular job, the energised volunteer is internally – or in today's psychological terms, intrinsically – motivated at a very high level. Money, or hope of promotion, is not what drives them.

Their buzz comes partly from their involvement in the cause they are contributing to. And it is also partly due to the **autonomy** involved. It is their choice, their decision, to contribute.

This is important for two reasons. First, it gives confidence, a sense of self-worth, and energy to the giver. Second, it tends to induce a sense of genuine gratitude in the receiver of the service offered.

The relationship between a recipient of help from someone who is paid to do the job or is a half-hearted volunteer there through duty (they are on a par), and someone who is doing it voluntarily because they want to give back is immeasurably different.

A personal experience recently underlined this.

For the past twenty years or so as a prison visitor and mentor, I have sat with sex offenders, multiple murderers, drug traffickers and others, first in Wandsworth, and subsequently in Wormwood Scrubs, both large London prisons. I have got, and still get, a real sense of fulfilment from doing this. And I have learned a lot in the process.

After the first few sessions with a prisoner, the outpourings of self-denial and self-justification tend to dry up. They are replaced by more honesty and more humanity. The true (or truer) backstory emerges. Many of the prisoners have been horribly abused as children. Many can't read or write and have very poor education. And many are fighting a drugs or alcohol habit. Most slowly reveal their hurt, and their desire to be more conventional members of society. And more loved.

The fact you are a willing volunteer changes your relationship with the person or persons you are trying to help. The recent experience that confirmed this for me took place during a visit I made to a new prisoner whom I was to mentor.

Getting into a prison to make a visit takes time. Not just the journey there, but the performance of getting through security at the gate, and then locked door by locked door that clangs behind you as you find your way to a room in one of the wings. When I eventually got there, the prisoner I was to meet refused to see me, saying he was in a meeting with other prisoners discussing an education programme he was on. I pressed, but still the message came back – he was busy.

As you can imagine, I was disappointed by his reaction. I relayed this to the people running the mentoring service in the prison. He didn't seem to understand, or wasn't interested, in the process, which involved establishing a relationship while he was in prison, and then meeting him from time to time to provide emotional and psychological support – and even practical advice on finding housing or employment – once he was released.

A short while afterwards I learned he was deeply apologetic, and that he did want to see me. I went to talk to him. It transpired that he had turned me away because he thought I was a prison employee, and that I was just ticking another box in the rigmarole of his release. Once he realised I was a volunteer, with no agenda, he was very keen to meet me and talk about his situation.

The point of this anecdote is to illustrate that as a volunteer you are in a special relationship with the individual being helped. This is because you are (or should be) giving freely of your time and of yourself, and you are your own person. You are unlikely to be a hireling of the organisation or a begrudging volunteer, so you will be an agenda-free zone.

As anyone receiving help will concur, you can smell people with an agenda at fifty paces.

This puts you – as a person without an agenda – in a privileged position. Privileged, because you can more rapidly build up trust than paid employees (who are regarded as box tickers). Trust is the basis of any relationship that is going to work.

Yes, a fast track to trust can be a surprising but significant benefit of autonomy.

2. GIVING THROUGH PHILANTHROPY

The most straightforward form of giving is direct philanthropy. Donating money to an individual, a movement or a cause is worthwhile and seems easy.

But it's not always that easy.

Even a simple one-to-one donation in the street – giving to a homeless person asking for money – is complicated. The arguments in your head might go thus: *'This person needs help. I can give something that will marginally reduce their need.' 'Yes, but most homeless organisations counsel that giving is wrong. It reduces self-respect and any desire for self-help to improve their situation.' 'Yes, but even if this person is conning me, he or she still probably has less than I do, and they're freezing cold sitting there.' 'They'll only spend it on drugs or alcohol, making their situation worse.' 'At least drugs or alcohol will give them a small release from their misery.'*

And so on.

Wherever you look it tends to be complicated. Giving to charities operating in disaster zones or famine relief also has challenges. Where are the blankets being sourced? Are the relief goods putting local tradespeople out of business? Is too much of the money being syphoned off by corrupt local officials?

I remember being appalled at finding out how much the managers of a well-known charity were paid, and how much they were spending on going to conferences, entertaining each other in plush hotels, when the charity concerned was meant to be helping the displaced and destitute.

I later spoke to a friend who had recently joined the charity sector to find that even that was not as simple as it seemed. Charities, she said, had to employ well-paid professionals and go to global conferences, otherwise they wouldn't be seen as serious. Which meant they wouldn't get funding from governments and the major trust funds and foundations. These large funders couldn't risk putting money into charities run on a shoestring that might not be here tomorrow, let alone in five years' time. It made sense.

The fact that it's not easy shouldn't put you off.

There are many reasons why not, but two are paramount. One is that – as all religions counsel – it is profoundly right to share what you have with the less advantaged.

It's not just 'There but for the grace of God, go I,' which is in a sense like paying a kind of insurance premium against a potential future personal misfortune. Giving spontaneously to help others less fortunate is different. It is a generous, empathetic response. We understand and we feel their pain. So we give. It confirms our humanity.

The second reason is that globally governments are overburdened with debt and finding it very difficult to balance the books. Austerity in one form or another therefore looks set to be with us for some time to come. So having adequate, let alone generous, social security budgets is likely to be a real challenge.

This means governments' contributions to the social sector will continue to shrink. This in turn means the other players in the social sector – especially the charities – will have to pick up the burden governments have let fall.

So charities are having to take up an increasing amount of slack. It is crucial they do, because they also provide much of the infrastructure for volunteering. If charities and social enterprises aren't well funded, they won't be able to provide the mechanisms for volunteers to work in disaster relief, reducing the isolation of the elderly, running the Lifeboat service, providing a Friends service in hospitals, or any of the other excellent services provided by volunteers.

So philanthropy is vital in providing money for direct use – in looking for cures for diseases like cancer, or relieving poverty at home and abroad – but also to supply the means for us to volunteer to give of ourselves in one-to-one human contact.

3. GIVING THROUGH RECOGNITION

One of the major motivators in organisations – and life in general – is recognition. We all yearn to be appreciated for what we do, and who we are. A pat on the back, a 'thank you' is often reward enough for prodigious effort on our part.

Not to be recognised can result in our being dispirited or even resentful. Recognition, on the other hand, fires us up, and confirms our sense of self-worth. A whole industry has built up in order to find ways to recognise people. From the Oscars at one end of the spectrum to Salesperson of the Month at the other, a multiplicity of prizes, awards, cups, titles and badges have been developed to congratulate people for their contributions and achievements.

The power of recognition is equally strong – and equally important – person to person.

There is a definitive short book on the subject, which I highly recommend. It is David Dunn's *Try Giving Yourself Away*. The book was written in the early 1920s. There have been frequent updates and new editions along the way, and it still retains its charm and relevance.

The central idea is that you make a *hobby* of giving yourself away, and that the most effective way of doing this is to recognise the efforts and contributions of others. His hobby takes many forms – praising, thanking, celebrating and congratulating his fellow citizens, his family and anyone else he can find to recognise for a kind deed or a worthwhile effort.

An uplifting book, it brings to life the joy and effectiveness of the act of recognition. It is, as I say, short, but packed with wisdom and folksy examples of that wisdom in action. A must-read if you are serious about embracing true generosity of spirit. Dunn is, however, clear-eyed about it. He makes the point strongly that all thanks or praise must be honest and justified. Any puffery or flattery would be insincere and will backfire.

He also condemns reckless giving at the expense of the financial wellbeing of one's family. Mrs Jellyby, the 'telescopic philanthropist' in Dickens's *Bleak House*, who raised money for the poor in Africa while her own children starved at her feet, would have received short shrift from Dunn.

For him, giving away just for its own sake brings happiness: 'today's giveaway is a blind investment in future happiness'.

4. GIVING BY BEING THERE

As a Second Biter you will still be leading a highly active life, and finding time to slow down can be the most challenging aspect of giving.

It means you may need to make a considerable effort to adjust to the pace of a sick or elderly person. Or to have the patience to help your grandchildren with their homework. But 'really being there' and genuinely giving them your full attention is not easy. You want to finish the sentence, give an opinion, hurry on, when all the person wants is for you to be there and listen. They don't want input; they want companionship and understanding. They don't want your opinions and your insights; they want your time and your friendship.

And time for the person you're helping is often their enemy. It stretches endlessly in front of them, with very little to fill it. They may be lonely, they may have lost their companions or their partner, and you are one of the only connections they have to a world of living flesh and blood, rather than that seen through a TV screen. While you are with them, time starts to move again. They are once more connected. And you need to be, too.

As we get older, one major opportunity that will only multiply, and is therefore worth highlighting, is in the giving back of a little time to the carers of people with incapacitating conditions like cancer or dementia.

Carers are the unsung heroes of our society. They give selflessly to the person they are caring for, and are often themselves becoming exhausted – and ill – from the effort. For the carer, time is in very short supply – they seldom have enough to guarantee their physical and mental health, let alone any time on their own to reground themselves.

Their sleep is often interrupted by the person they are caring for, and some can't even use the toilet in peace. Giving such a person time off – a morning, a day, even a day and a night – can be a gift of generosity on your part, and of huge value to the recipient.

Sitting and listening to the carer him or herself may be just as beneficial as listening to the person being cared for. Everyone needs to talk, to communicate, and sometimes to complain. A sympathetic and non-judgemental ear on your part can work wonders.

Just remember that like all time-giving, it needs to be an unrushed and fully listening ear. One that is totally 'there'.

SAYING NO CAN BE GENEROUS

Saying no can also be a generous win/win. As someone who is enthusiastic, and gets things done, you may be asked to give in many ways – especially of your time. Other people may not understand that you don't have acres of unfilled hours at your disposal.

So, however tempting, and whatever the pressure, if you haven't got the time or the inclination to make a good job of it, say no. You will avoid frustration on the part of the receiver and yourself.

Another reason to decline is that if you say yes and don't have the time to do a good job, you are effectively giving away autonomy. You are letting their timetable dictate to you, and you are powerless to turn it round. Frustration on your part will turn to anxiety. You will be in thrall to guilt. So say NO.

5. GIVING THROUGH GENERAL GOODNESS

'A person who is consistently kind is a person with humility.

'In being kind, no matter what, she chooses not to create separation by tearing others down. Her kindness demonstrates respect. It shows that she knows that she shares her humanity with everyone she interacts with. It even shows confidence: by extending a hand

to another, in ways big and small, whenever she can, she shows
that she knows that raising others up doesn't cost anything, doesn't
use up any scarce resource.

'Kindness is abundance manifest.'

– Sasha Dichter, Acumen

Kindness is certainly a key manifestation of General Goodness, a catch-all phrase that incorporates the many ways you can give.

Here are a few more ways of giving:

- Your time (to individuals rather than to a cause or a charity)
- Your skill
- Your love
- Your commitment
- Your wisdom
- Your enthusiasm
- Your generosity
- Your energy
- Your support
- Your expertise
- Your trust
- Your caring
- Your humanity
- Your understanding
- Your sympathy
- Your presence
- Your friendship.

You have a wealth of human attributes to give.

The great thing about giving, as David Dunn pointed out – whatever form it takes – is that it is a win/win. The giver and the receiver are both rewarded. Both feel good about it. It's like Christmas presents. It's usually at least as much fun and as satisfying to give as to receive them.

GIVING IS PART OF PERSONAL GROWTH – AS WELL AS FUELLING THE AUTONOMIES

We've seen that giving not only helps the recipients, but it brings many benefits to the givers too.

Beyond the rewards we've looked at, giving can contribute to and accelerate very real personal growth. In giving, you will be engaged and probably challenged as an individual. You may have to leave your comfort zone, especially if your job did not involve interacting with people in need of succour and support. You'll hit challenges and have to problem-solve.

In the words of Yvon Chouinard, mountaineer and the founder of Patagonia, the outdoor-clothing company, 'It's not an adventure till something goes wrong'. And as Kurt Hahn clearly understood, it is in overcoming these challenges of something going wrong that character is built.

So, giving involves growing and learning. And in the process it enhances our capacity to earn as well.

Giving brings with it so many ways to learn – how different people live, how to help solve their problems, how you can help more generally, how to be present, and new skills needed to do so. And because you have to bring more of yourself in order to do that genuinely – for it to be effectively received and realised – you are more open as a person and vulnerable too. As a result, your *capability* to learn is also enhanced.

Personal vulnerability makes you both more grounded and more empathetic with strangers. This can be crucial when you're trying to start earning in more creative ways. You will be more attuned to the needs of potential customers, and more sensitive to opportunities that arise to create relevant value for them.

Interestingly, enlightened employers understand that personal development is an important part of professional development, and many encourage employees to volunteer.

Finally, Second Biters need to be able to cope with bumps along the trail. Feeling good about yourself gives you a solid sense of self-confidence. We've touched on it and many books have been written on confidence – and I'm sure they contain helpful wisdom – but there can be little more confidence-building activity than understanding and appreciating that you are doing something generous and worthwhile.

So the rewards will more than compensate for the difficult bits. Whether it is volunteering, giving to causes that resonate with you, making time for people, or generally doing good, you will feel that you are making a difference, fulfilling your potential by helping others to fulfil theirs.

SO, GO GIVE

All four autonomies – Earning, Learning, Giving and Recharging – have a positive interplay between them. Autonomy by definition is self-centred – it's taking control of your surroundings and

your life – but generosity can, and should, play a crucial and wonderful role within it.

Your reward will be an uplifting sense of 'Yes, this is what I ought to be doing. This feels right. And so do I'. Not to mention those other benefits of an enhanced immune system, more energy, a feeling of mastery – and even weight loss.

So, what's stopping you?

GET YOUR MOUTH WATERING FOR YOUR
SECOND BITE OF THE CHERRY

Let's consolidate what you might have learned in this chapter:

1. Put 'health benefits of volunteering' or 'health benefits of giving' into a search engine and you'll have hours of happy reading. The studies quoting the evidence of the positive effects on physical and mental health are overwhelming. Not to mention social health, as it counteracts isolation and loneliness.

2. Check out charities working in fields or geographies that interest you. Explore their websites; try to find someone who can give you the inside track, and talk to them.

3. Separately, look at websites for volunteering, such as csv.org.uk, yearofthevolunteer.org or charitychoice.co.uk.

Ideas to explore this element further:

1. To be good at giving, it helps to be good at receiving, and being *grateful*. They are two sides of the same coin. Two exercises:
   a. Jot down a few things you are profoundly grateful for.
   b. When being thanked for something you have done or given, accept graciously, no mumbling.

2. Get hold of a copy of David Dunn's *Try Giving Yourself Away* and read it through.

3. Practise saying, 'No. I'd love to, but terribly sorry, I can't'.

CHAPTER SEVEN

AUTONOMY FOUR – RECHARGING

*'People are like electricity. They work better when
they are switched on.'*

– Peter Drucker, ultra-wise management guru

**SEVEN INSIDIOUS EXCUSES FORCEFULLY REJECTED
BY HIGHLY EFFECTIVE PEOPLE**

EXCUSE NO.5

**I'm having a rest. No deadlines. No pressure. Leave me
alone.**

By all means include rest and relaxation in your lifestyle.
You may need (and even deserve) a break, but keep
it short. Too much time spent lotus eating and indulging
yourself can reduce your internal dynamo to almost
zero.

This autonomy is about recharging your batteries so you can enjoy,
and even revel, in life. That means being at the top of your game
mentally, physically and even spiritually.

It's about *enjoying* yourself, and your spare time in a way that balances and enhances your other autonomies.

Of course, while some of the edges of the autonomies blur and overlap, recharging is also about the judicious and enjoyable use of your leisure time in order to ensure you have energy to spare for Earning, Giving and Learning.

The chapter will cover several approaches to this. But remember, the whole idea of autonomy is that *you* decide.

So choose the things that will, or might, work for you, and don't worry about the others. Bear in mind that you as an individual are constantly growing and changing, so you may find one or two of the rejects this time around might be very relevant later.

THE AVOIDANCE OF MIND-ROT

Sitting in an armchair or lying on a recliner on a beach is great. Life has been hectic, you deserve a rest.

But sloth is one of the deadly sins, and for good reason. It involves spiritual and emotional apathy, not just being lazy. Apathy is about consciously or unconsciously disengaging from life, and ending up as a physical and mental slob.

Slobbing out is a short-term – and often very enjoyable – event. But it should not become an occupation or the mind will truly start to rot. Remember, you are either growing or you are dying. And extended lotus eating comes firmly into the latter category.

Stimulation of the mind is necessary, just as stimulation of the body is desirable to keep the body functioning. As with most things in life, it's about a balance. A balance between the *recovery/reward* aspects of what you do in your spare time, and the *stimulus/*

re-energising aspects: when to sit in a deckchair or when to climb a mountain. Together they make up the Recharging Autonomy – and as such it's your decision where the balance lies.

How you balance it will change over time, and will also be influenced by events. It's just worth bearing in mind as you make your decision that the growing/dying principle holds good for energy, too. The more you do, the more energy you have to do things. The less you do, the more tired and listless you are. You decide.

Recreation, (re-creating ourselves) and thus recharging our batteries, falls for the purposes of this book into four main areas: physical, and various dimensions of mental, or cognitive, activity. Let's examine each of them.

1. PHYSICAL RECHARGING

When I was at school, I was reasonably academic, but I used to live for physical recreation. I would look out of the window at the pupils enjoying their sport or games and yearn to be out there with them. I loved break time, when I could get outside with my fellow students and kick a ball around the playground.

I still retain this physical need for exercise, and am lucky enough to be able to run, swim, play tennis and go to the gym. If I do nothing, my body feels like an unflushed toilet. Exercise seems to cleanse both my body and mind. Even if, on a cold, unwelcoming winter's day I would rather not go out, I still do, and am always glad later that I made the effort.

I realise most people are not like this. Some, indeed, loathe organised exercise. But the fact is that medical science is universally of the opinion that exercise and diet are two of the key contributors to both a healthy life and a long life. So for the vast majority of people, some kind of exercise is plainly beneficial.

And it's worth remembering that it takes twenty-one days of continuous practice to form a habit. So in three weeks' time you could have built the habit of exercise.

But there's more to physical recharging than just exercise. The work done on Blue Zones is an interesting indicator of what makes up a life that combines health with longevity.

Blue Zones identify demographic and/or geographic areas in the world where people live measurably longer, healthier lives. Of course, genes play an important part in longevity (though only accounting for 10 per cent according to some studies), and there's not a lot we can do about that. What the Blue Zones studies show is that there are several ways we *can* impact increased health and longevity. They are as follows:

- Take regular exercise (tick)
- Eat a diet rich in vegetables, fruit and herbs
- Only drink alcohol in moderation
- Build and maintain a social network of family and friends
- Attend religious services, if you are religious.

The research also found two other elements that impacted on health and longevity. Not smoking, and, if at all possible, living in a community or society that has a reasonable degree of social equality and where people look out for each other.

Diet is on the list, and is obviously important in being healthy. You can't argue with fruit and vegetables being nutritious. More interesting (and it crops up in other research) are the results of the **80 per cent full rule**.

Participants in Blue Zones, and in similar studies, whether consciously or not, have formulas to stop eating when feeling only 80 per cent replete. The reason is that it takes twenty minutes for the stomach to get the message through to the brain that you are in fact full. So they avoid overeating, obesity and the associated health problems.

The stratagems needed to achieve this vary. Some cultures avoid people helping themselves to more food by serving out just sufficient onto individual dishes, and then putting the food away, so seconds are not on offer. Others consciously use smaller plates, so there is less food on them (a very effective technique for reducing alcohol consumption, by the way – use smaller glasses).

If exercise is unavoidable for health in general, and our later years in particular – and it would seem to be – what kind of exercise qualifies?

The good news for people who hate the thought of sweaty exercise or sport of any kind is that exercise is a broad church. The Blue Zone long and healthy lifers tend to do no sport at all and virtually no systematised exercise. Their physical workouts are entirely natural. They are part of their normal lifestyles.

Most are still active and have no concept of retirement. They are farmers, shepherds and cooks without kitchen appliances, so there is plenty of chopping and stirring. They walk everywhere (and frequently) and garden actively. They are constantly on the go and there is no sense of grinding out an exercise routine.

The lesson is that exercise should be enjoyable and feel like it is recharging you, so it doesn't have to look or feel like exercise. Golf, yoga, carpentry, gardening and walking, to name but a few, all qualify. And there is no need to undertake a walking holiday as if you were on a training camp for Olympic glory. It can be just as effective, and probably more fun, if it also involves quite a bit of talking with new or old friends and stopping frequently to enjoy the view.

2. COGNITIVE RECHARGING: BRAIN FUNCTION

'Besides his memory decays,
He recollects not what he says;
He cannot call his friends to mind;
Forgets the place where last he dined:
Plies you with stories o'er and o'er,
He told them fifty times before.
How does he fancy we can sit,
To hear his out-of-fashion wit?
But he takes up with younger folks,
Who for his wine will bear his jokes:
Faith, he must make his stories shorter,
Or change his comrades once a quarter.'

– Jonathan Swift, 1667–1745

It is widely recognised that there is brain function fall-off with age. This includes some aspects of memory, multitasking ability, and information-processing speed. The poem above shows that Swift, the great satirist and author of *Gulliver's Travels*, certainly appreciated it even in the early part of the eighteenth century. What is less recognised is that this doesn't usually begin until you are in your seventies.

Indeed, abstract thinking ability and inductive reasoning are all at their peak in the years between thirty-nine and the late sixties. This means that key skills like the ability to identify solutions, to implement a plan and to find ways to work with other people are at their highest level during this period.

So we're not past it yet. In fact older people, in psychology-speak, have higher levels of crystallised intelligence (though perform less well on measures of fluid intelligence). This, translated, means older people have more general knowledge and broader experiences, which gives them more insight and understanding, so decision-making is better too.

'In sum, if we define wisdom as knowledge combined with its judicious use, then older people seem to have it, well into retirement. Moreover, this wisdom may more than compensate for what they lack in other areas.'

– Thomas T. Hills, Ph.D., professor of psychology at the University of Warwick, writing on The Myth of Age-Related Cognitive Decline

What does this mean for us and our Recharging autonomy? That first up, we're starting from a strong place –– we're likely to be better brain-wise than we and others often assume. But there are also things we can do to improve matters.

The news for sudoku and crossword enthusiasts is good to mixed. It is certainly worth enjoying such regular brain challenges, and 'use it or lose it' does apply to several areas, including numeracy.

I can attest to this. When I started up in business on my own, working from home in the early nineties, I did everything, including the bookkeeping, myself. In the early days I used mental arithmetic (checked later with a calculator) to do my VAT return. It took time, but it was somehow satisfying.

I then changed to a software package, which meant the tax return took about thirty seconds to process on the computer. Rapidly, my powers of numeracy declined. I comforted myself with the thought that the same thing would have happened if I had transferred to a computerised system in my twenties rather than my fifties. And I was probably right. Use it or lose it.

Nicholas Spitzer, professor of neuroscience at the University of California, and editor-in-chief of BrainFacts.org, has surveyed the evidence, and he is clear that crossword puzzles and games like sudoku do not enhance cognitive function overall. However, they can improve specific areas of brain performance: verbal aptitude and the ability to learn a new subject more quickly. Pretty big wins in anybody's book.

Significantly, he claims research is very clear on the two major drivers of improved brain performance: exercise and sunlight. Exercise, in particular, he says, helps the body to devote lots of resources to cognitive functions.

Focusing on a different tack of cognitive performance and the understanding of the brain is the relatively new science of neuroplasticity. This has been brought into the public domain by Norman Doidge, a professor of psychiatry at both the University of Toronto and the University of Columbia in New York.

Neuroplasticity is the science of the brain's ability to be reshaped. Plasticity just means the capacity to be re-formed into something new. The plastic arts – like sculpture – relate to a shape that has been transformed into something different, like a statue or similar artwork.

Previously it was believed that the brain was a fixed and non-regenerative organ. Once damaged by a disease such as Parkinson's, it could not be repaired. Doidge's second book, *The Brain's Way of Healing*, traces case histories of patients that have managed to rewire their brains. Not to repair them but create workarounds that achieve a similar effect.

What he argues, and demonstrates, is that mental activity can reshape the brain. This is exciting stuff. Neuroplasticity is in its infancy, but the potential of future developments to accelerate our understanding of the brain is potentially transformational.

Here is a science that could arrest, and even reverse, any decline in our brain function. It can't arrive too soon. In the meantime, it's worth finding brain exercises that are both fun (recovery/reward) as well as challenging (stimulus/recharging).

3. COGNITIVE RECHARGING: SOUL NOURISHMENT

Nourishing the soul is about finding uplift and inspiration.

Books, music, art, theatre can all bring us huge pleasure. At their best they involve and inspire us as human beings. We are engaged in a way that somehow transcends our daily existence and elevates our sensibility. To me, the impact of great art can have an almost spiritual quality. The here and now dissolves, and you feel in the presence of a timeless beauty.

I am not religious, but people who are will presumably appreciate this in a more intense form. The feeling is becoming stronger as I age, and this could be connected with an increasing sense of mortality. I don't think much about death – young people don't, and I still see myself as young – but if that is what is precipitating this increased enjoyment of beauty, then this is another reason to celebrate our mature years.

It may also be connected with the fact that I now participate in the foothills of meditation (see below). As a result I take more time to notice, and dwell on, things around me.

It is important to understand that we are privileged to live at a time when the availability of art and culture is at levels undreamed of in previous generations. High-quality music of all types is available at the press of a button. We can have Pavarotti sing for us all day. Even though he is no longer alive. We can listen to books on the train. We can witness great events on TV or online. We can take virtual tours of art galleries and museums.

Nothing, however, quite replaces *being* there. A Rembrandt in the flesh, or walking into St Mark's Square in Venice, are still breathtaking in a way a digital reproduction can't be. The shared experience of great opera at Covent Garden or the Metropolitan Opera House is hard to replicate, even in a cinema. But even the reproductions are a whole lot better than they used to be.

It needn't be high art, although I find I appreciate it more than I did when I was younger. Another benefit of being a Second Biter. One simple form of elevated enjoyment is taking time to enjoy food in the company of friends.

It is not without reason that the word *company* comes from the Latin *cum panis* – 'with bread'. Conviviality – sharing food – is a rich source of soul nourishment as well as bodily nourishment. Whether with family or friends, it is an elevated form of enjoyment and deeply satisfying.

Beyond food and company, I love reading. When you lose yourself in a book, you are there in real time. I think of the young boy, shortly after the introduction of television, who was asked by a reporter which he preferred – traditional radio, or the new medium of TV? His reply was radio. On being asked why, he replied, 'Because the pictures are better.' It's the same with books for me.

Today, the convenience of soul fodder is wonderful. We can have books delivered within hours of ordering them, and great art is now presented in galleries and museums in much more informative and accessible ways. We have the huge privilege of being able to feast ourselves on great culture.

And we are in control. We have autonomy. We decide what masterpieces we view or listen to. Great art used to be in the control of the wealthy and powerful. Now more and more, it is democratised, and made more accessible to all. We choose, we enjoy, we are recharged.

In addition to the soul nourishment provided by culture or food, there are many other manifestations. Three in which we have great autonomy are **Meditation, Breathing** and **Mindfulness**.

Meditation is the larger concept, and can include mindfulness (which can be practised on its own). Meditation is defined as separating the mind and body from thoughts and feelings in order to become fully aware. It is incorporated in almost all religions in one form or another.

As well as playing an important part as a component of religious contemplative practice, meditation is of course an important element in some versions of yoga. And increasingly it is used as a therapy for promoting good health and boosting the immune system. In essence, it means simply *being* – suspending thinking, being at peace, living in the moment.

Buddhists are probably the most widely recognised exponents of meditation. Their stages and forms of meditation are highly evolved, and highly effective. Emptying their minds of unhelpful or toxic thoughts, they move to a state of compassion that incorporates all living things.

The Buddhist priests I have encountered have been highly impressive human beings, full of unexpected humour as well as loving kindness. I've tried meditating in a group, and have found it very helpful. Owing to what is probably a lack of self-discipline on my part, and the fact that because of sporting injuries I find it difficult to find and stay comfortable in a meditational position, I have not, as yet, persevered and tried it on my own.

I would, however, recommend giving it a serious go. Its benefits in recharging are very real.

Within the wider canon of meditation, I personally practise two of the more immediately productive elements: breathing and mindfulness.

Breathing plays an important part in meditation, and as well as stilling the mind it has other health benefits (not the least of which is having a positive effect on high blood pressure). One of the key lessons to bear in mind is that **breathing out is more important than breathing in**. Interestingly, this correlates with medical advice I received when playing rugby. Our physiotherapist always told us at half-time to breathe out hard, as it was more important to push out the carbon dioxide than to breathe in oxygen.

Breathing is also a very effective way of reducing stress. It helps you feel more relaxed, focused and balanced. Several deep, controlled breaths before taking on a challenge, like speaking in public, can make a positive difference to your state of mind, and your performance. It can also be helpful during a sleepless patch in the night as a way of relaxing the mind and the body.

Mindfulness, or **Being in the Moment**, is a tool I find increasingly useful. Mindfulness is a simple yet powerful idea that is gaining more traction day by day. It is about being right here, right now, profoundly, and with no distractions.

The benefits are numerous and widely validated. Like all forms of meditation, it reduces stress, strengthens the immune system and increases wellbeing. It can even reduce pain levels, or at least raise pain thresholds so the pain is more tolerable. The extra plus from my point of view – and for many others – is that you don't have to go into training as a Buddhist monk for months and years to reap its rewards.

It's worth buying a book on mindfulness or going to classes to really get a handle on it. Distilled, the steps to achieving a superficial but helpful state of mindfulness are as follows:

- Sit down, relax and be intensely aware of each part of your body in turn – feet, legs, hips and so on.
- Be aware of your breath, but relax and don't be over aware of it.
- Breathe in and out from your belly (not your chest).
- Breathe in and out through your nose.
- Make your out breath longer than your in breath.
- Be aware of all your senses – Is it hot or cold? What sounds can you hear? What smells can you detect? What colours can you see? What shapes? What movements?
- Concentrate on being in the moment, so the past and the future cease to exist.
- If your mind drifts off, bring yourself gently back to your body.
- Come back to the everyday gently – no rush.

As you get into it, you can even practise on the move. I go each morning to the local newsagent to collect our morning paper. During my return I practise what is termed Mindful Walking. It sounds a bit odd but can be rewarding.

I concentrate on my feet then my legs until I am aware of them and their motion. I then tune into sounds, the temperature, and the shapes and colours around me. As I turn the corner towards home, I see the magnificent hundred-foot high trees in our local park. It is a sight of beauty and it sets me up for the day.

Finally, don't forget or underestimate exploring and enjoying *your own creativity* to feed the soul and recharge your mind.

Your own creativity is rich in potential, not just for re-energising yourself, but to find a significant degree of personal fulfilment. The field is unlimited – painting, creative writing, cooking, woodworking, sculpture, gardening, knitting, blogging, sketching, music, dancing, singing and so on.

And it includes simple creative *social* acts such as organising gatherings of friends, or meetings of people with a common interest. Organising young people to come together in a safe environment for sport or outdoor adventures can be fun as well as invigorating.

And creative activities can become important sources of income as well as satisfaction. Two of my friends have found this – one through woodworking, the other in sculpture. This really is a win/win/win. Creative activity such as this stimulates, recharges, fulfils, delights and rewards, all at the same time.

Getting started can be daunting, whether it is a creative pursuit you once enjoyed but have let lie, or beginning something anew. Going to classes or courses, be they life-drawing or creative writing, can be a good way to break the ice. Whatever kind, or kinds, of creative activity you undertake – and do give several a try – the psychological and soul rewards can be significant.

4. COGNITIVE RECHARGING: ATTITUDE

This is a big and important subject, and we will return to it in the next chapter. Its relevance here is in the two areas of openness and association, both of which can affect your capacity to recharge your other autonomies.

Openness is something that can decline with age. It is crucial to retain it – and if possible to increase it – because it is an *enabler and* *reinforcer* of all the autonomies. Openness to ideas and to people is what allows you to enjoy and benefit from rapid change, and the richness the evolving world has to offer.

Nothing stands still, and if you close down your mind and resist anything new or different, you are in for trouble. Not immediately, because it can be attractive to retreat into a comfort zone and resist all newcomers. Pull the blanket up over your head and snuggle into the familiarity of opinions and thinking that are past their use-by date.

The trouble comes when your closed attitude hits things like social media, or the evolving landscape of business and social enterprise start-ups. If your mind is shut, and your thinking is rooted in the world of work or the expectations of people twenty years ago, you will struggle to understand let alone take advantage of the opportunities available to Second Biters. The same goes for the ways to give and learn.

If you have reached this far in the book, it is highly likely you are open to change, and new ideas, and to meeting new people. The challenge is to ensure you stay that way.

As we shall see in Chapter 8, attitudes like openness can transcend age. The figures show that some people go into a cognitive decline in later years, and close down their thinking and consequently their horizons. But others – and you will be one – retain their openness, and flourish as a result.

Association – the people you associate with – is another important factor important in recharging your brain and your recharging capacity.

'*You are the average of the five people you spend most time with*'

– Jim Rohn

The words of Jim Rohn, one of the giants of the American personal development industry, hit the bullseye. The people you associate with have a massive effect on how you behave, how you think and even who you are. The influence on your attitudes and thinking by those close to you is little appreciated or recognised.

Worst of all is the effect negative people can have. Toxic people spread their poison, and it is very hard to resist. You get pulled down to their level of negativity. The only effective antidote is to move on and leave the toxic person behind.

This can be easier said than done. If the toxic person in your life is close to you, it's obviously a difficult, and wearing, situation. The best outcome is probably to try to contain their negativity by shutting it out as much as possible, so neutralising their chatterings, and to find other – highly positive people – to be in your life alongside them.

Going back to the Blue Zones mentioned earlier (see pages 123–5), one of the other key discriminators of the high concentration of the very elderly living healthy, active lives was *the tribe they were part of* (i.e. the people they associated with).

Indeed, the Framingham Cohort Studies, which took place in the US over a long period of time, have also indicated that the tribes people associate with are crucial to their health. Smokers tend to associate with smokers, obese people with obese people, and so on.

In the words of Benjamin Hapgood Burt's 1930s classic song of the drunkard's journey home from the bar …

My poor feet began to stutter
So I lay down in the gutter
And a pig came up and lay down by my side
Then we sang 'It's All Fair Weather'

And 'Good Fellows Get Together'
Till a lady passing by was heard to say
She says, 'You can tell a man who boozes
By the company he chooses'
And the pig got up and slowly walked away.

Importantly, back in the world of sobriety, happy people associate with happy people, and the conclusion is that associating with the right people can do more than almost anything else to positively affect your mental and physical health.

So the people you associate with are crucial to creating and confirming your attitudes and approach to life. It's therefore worth seriously considering the following as your personal Tribe Objectives over the coming months and years.

Spend as much time as possible with:

1. People you love, and who are positive
2. People who are younger than you (don't underestimate the power of this)
3. People who are warm-hearted
4. People with a sense of humour
5. Anyone who is uplifting and inspirational
6. Avoid – if humanely possible – toxic people.

This is about consciously assembling – and editing – the people around you. It may sound a bit manipulative, but why let serendipity run your life? You've reached a stage when decisive action on this, and the other fronts being considered here, could transform your life for the better.

'Keep away from people who try to belittle your ambitions.
Small people always do that, but the really great make you feel
that you, too, can somehow become great.'

– Mark Twain

RECHARGING, THE AUTONOMIES AND WORK/LIFE BALANCE

So Recharging is about using your leisure time constructively and creatively. And, of course, enjoyably. Doing so will leave you with energy to spare for the other autonomies.

There are inevitable overlaps. Reading, for instance, might come into both Learning and Recharging. It is a very pleasurable activity, and it stimulates and informs at the same time. Studying teaching methods to best help people with disabilities could cover both Learning and Giving. Similarly, when it creates both pleasure and energy, Recharging has an overlap with Learning, and Giving.

Just as it's up to you to decide how to split your recreation between *relaxing/rewarding* and *stimulating/re-energising*, the amount of time spent in each of the autonomies is also, of course, up to you. It will vary according to your circumstances, and where you are on your Second Bite trajectory. You may want to spend more days in a week in Learning and Recharging than Earning or Giving. Or vice versa. Or if you are involved in an engrossing and worthwhile project, it might be you devote six or even seven days to that. Being autonomous, you are in control.

The point is that if you can get all the autonomies working together, the synergy created virtually does away with the need for work/life balance as a concept.

You will not be trying to fit in your life around the constraints of work implied in the work/life divide. As a Second Biter, there will be gutty bits when things are tough in work, say, or volunteering – life is never tidy – but overall your life will be in balance. All four autonomies will be working in sync.

You will be making the choices. You will have energy from the sense of being in control, and the stress will be positive and manageable, not negative and anxiety-inducing. Not only will you have energy, your enthusiasm will be channelled towards activities that are worthwhile and uplifting. It will be a virtuous circle. Your life will be self-balancing.

GET YOUR MOUTH WATERING FOR YOUR
SECOND BITE OF THE CHERRY

Let's consolidate what you might have learned in this chapter:

1. Watch Jonathan Sackner Bernstein, electrical engineer turned cardiologist, turned polymath and difference-maker, on the TEDx talk: tedxtalks.ted.com/video/It-s-not-too-late-to-make-a-dif You'll find out how mentally sharp you still are and how you can still make a difference. Even if you are over seventy, like me. There's also some great stuff on older people founding successful companies.

2. Watch Dan Buettner explaining Blue Zones and living to be 100 plus: ted.com/talks/dan_buettner_how_to_live_to_be_100 Or check out one of the summaries: bluezonesproject.com/bluezones

3. Read and think about the implications of Norman Doidge's books *The Brain that Changes Itself* and *The Brain's Way of Healing*.

Ideas to explore this element further:

1. Read *Do Breathe: Calm your mind. Find focus. Get stuff done* by Michael Townsend Williams. Excellent on all three areas, it's a really worthwhile read.

2. Exercise – it helps you to sleep better, so you will recharge better.

3. Read *You Can't afford the Luxury of a Negative Thought* by John Roger and Peter McWilliams, a pop classic on positive thinking. It's pretty pop but very well worth reading. And acting on.

CHAPTER EIGHT

MINDSETS IN GENERAL (AND THE AUTONOMY MINDSET IN PARTICULAR)

'Mindsets are just beliefs. They're powerful beliefs but they're just something in your mind, and you can change your mind.'

– Carole Dweck, 'Mindset'

SEVEN INSIDIOUS EXCUSES FORCEFULLY REJECTED BY HIGHLY EFFECTIVE PEOPLE

EXCUSE NO.6

It's OK for me to moan about how bad society is becoming. I've earned the right.

It's not OK at all. First, it's not true (older generations always think things were better in their day). Second, moaning is mentally damaging and creates excuses for doing nothing.

Mindsets are things we are often not aware we have: it's just how we are used to seeing the world. And often that perspective is not only unconscious but unhelpful too. It prevents us from appreciating our talents and blinkers us from seeing our opportunities.

A positive mindset, on the other hand, can make anything possible. In order for us to really understand mindset change, it's worth looking at how they can affect not only our outlooks and attitudes but also our *behaviour*. Let's look at some tangible examples. We'll start with a global mindset that people were happy with for many years. Until someone pointed out it was outdated, false, cruel and repulsive.

CHANGING A GLOBAL MINDSET

In the late-eighteenth and early-nineteenth centuries, the world economy depended on slavery to function efficiently. It was accepted wisdom that without slaves to cut the sugarcane or pick the cotton, or do whatever menial jobs need doing, developed economies would falter and collapse.

It was believed that if labour had to be paid for, staple goods would be unaffordable in mass markets, volumes would shrink rapidly, and widespread financial ruin would ensue. But the accepted wisdom was not reality.

The necessity of slavery for the smooth functioning of the world economy was a mindset adopted, possibly unconsciously, by the wealthy merchants and landowners of the time. And it was confirmed by those involved in international commerce generally. Slavery was convenient, efficient and good for the bottom line.

But over time, the practice was questioned by a small minority that became alarmed at its de-humanising cruelty and scale. As the years passed, this minority became more vocal, strengthened and inspired by brave activists amongst those enslaved. Eventually these voices reached Parliament, where a sum of money in the tens of millions of pounds was voted through to buy off the commercial interests that claimed they depended on the practice to survive; they had to be *bribed* to do the right thing.

Slavery was abolished in the UK in 1833 and it was the American Civil War thirty years later that finally saw it abolished in the US. Neither economy collapsed.

The point is that this lynchpin of the economy wasn't a lynchpin at all. It was just a *mindset* that said it was. And mindsets are perspectives that are adopted, consciously or unconsciously, that can change or be changed. And changed on a global scale, even though at the time they appear to be the only reasonable way of looking at things.

A modern example of mindset evolution, followed by behavioural change, would be our attitudes to climate change and the need for recycling. There is a long way to go before there is significant climate change, but at least we have begun that journey.

CHANGING A LOCAL MINDSET

Changing mindsets on a local scale can be transformational too.

The Dutch football team of Ajax developed a new mindset for its players in the late 1960s and early 1970s. It led to the club winning the European Cup in 1971, 1972 and 1973, and to the national Netherlands side getting to the final of the World Cup in 1974.

Until this time, the players played in positions that suited their physical attributes and also their psychological outlook. They were forwards, midfielders or defenders, and seldom tried a different position. The goalkeeper, of course, who could use his hands, was even more rooted between his goalposts.

The breakthrough in mindset came when the coaches developed what came to be called Total Football. This tactical theory involved all the players learning to play in each other's positions. Defenders, midfielders and forwards all got first-hand experience of their teammates' roles – their needs and their opportunities.

This had several benefits. Each player had a better understanding of how they could help each other in their different roles. They had a greater spatial awareness of the different parts of the field and how they interrelated. And they could interchange roles during a game. This gave more flexibility and dynamism, as well as confusing the opposition.

Total Football, by giving each player a more open, creative and fluid mindset, supercharged the success of both the individual players and the team as a whole. And the concept quickly spread, influencing players and coaches around the world.

CHANGING BUSINESS/ORGANISATION/INDUSTRY MINDSETS

Many organisations in the nineties adopted the practice of setting what was called *Big Hairy Audacious Goals* (BHAG). You might have been involved in a few yourself. For those of you not familiar with it, the objective of this kind of goal setting is to shake up and shift people's thinking, from a mindset that is based solely on improving performance by an achievable amount each year.

This little-by-little approach, based on the Japanese practice of continuous, incremental improvement (Kaizen), is a great philosophy but has a tendency to lure people into a comfort zone of taking small steps. With the rapid and seismic changes in technology and market structures in today's world, it can be dangerous as it can lure organisations into a deluded sense of security.

Big Hairy Audacious Goals are a way of getting people to reframe their thinking in an exciting and challenging way. *Mindsets are changed, a new and bigger picture comes into focus and behaviours change.*

PAUL POLMAN, CEO OF UNILEVER,
TALKING TO *McKINSEY QUARTERLY*, **MAY 2014:**

'The first thing is mindset. When I became chief executive, in 2009, I said, "We are going to double our turnover." People hadn't heard that message for a long time, and it helped get back what I call their "growth mindset". You simply cannot save your way to prosperity. The second thing was about the way we should grow. We made it very clear that we needed to think differently about the use of resources and to develop a more inclusive growth model. So we created the Unilever Sustainable Living Plan, which basically says that we will double our turnover, reduce our absolute environmental impact, and increase our positive social impact.

Because it takes a longer-term model to address these issues, I decided we wouldn't give guidance any more and would stop full reporting on a quarterly basis; we needed to remove the temptation to work only towards the next set of numbers [...] Thinking for the long term

> has removed enormous shackles from our organisation. I really believe that's part of the strong success we have seen over the past five years.'

Big Hairy Audacious Goals is popular in many organisations for the reason that it gives those people setting the goals and buying into them a sense of *ownership* of the future. They buy into the longer-term plans of the company.

This is commendable, but it can also have the side-effect of increasing levels of stress in the organisation. Because ownership and autonomy are separate and different things, it has the effect of producing the following equation:

Responsibility minus autonomy = increased stress

The challenge all organisations have, whether they be commercial, governmental or whatever, is that employee engagement is largely enabled and supercharged by giving people autonomy. But – and it's a big but – the complexity of modern life means that giving genuine autonomy to employees is deemed too much of a risk.

But it's not always been the case. Bank managers used to rely on judgement honed by experience when deciding whether or not to give a company or individuals a loan or an overdraft. Now an algorithm, largely without human intervention, does it. Some of the more successful organisations, especially in the service industries, do succeed in giving front-line employees a measure of autonomy. But the autonomy is generally within tightly prescribed parameters. It's not real autonomy: it's pat-on-the-head autonomy.

Occasionally, there are mavericks amongst the employees, who can work autonomously within the system. If they don't get fired, they generally end up as the CEO. Some do pull it off, and they deserve a heartfelt round of applause.

Even judges can change their mindsets

The US, like many countries, has a problem with ex-service people (or 'veterans', as they call them) readjusting to civilian life. Many suffer from understandable mental health problems such as Post Traumatic Stress Disorder in one form or another after seeing and experiencing things in military engagements that are horrific – and – what is so damaging – which occur relentlessly day after day, and week after week. After leaving the service, life without structure – and possibly purpose – can be very tough. Problems with drugs and alcohol abound. Veterans make up nearly a fifth of all homeless people in the US, and a similar 20 per cent of all suicides.

In 2008, Robert Russell, a judge in Buffalo, New York, seeing so many veterans come before him, adjusted his mindset on how he viewed these 'troublemakers'. He set up a special Veterans' Treatment Court, which deals with people with substance abuse, alcohol and mental health issues, giving them treatment support, training and housing. Each person is given a mentor (also a veteran) who supplies help, and tough love if necessary. If they take the treatment and pass the tests, and shape up generally, their sentences can be reduced or even dismissed. The course lasts at least a year, and those succeeding have been known to get a standing ovation from the judge.

> Many other courts are now following suit, as the recidivism figures are dramatically lower than that of other systems or incarceration. By changing his mindset in the treatment of veterans and their misdemeanours, Judge Russell has changed the lives of countless veterans for the better.

THE CHALLENGE: RETHINKING *YOUR* MINDSET

Of course, we all tend to think our own mindset is the correct one, as that is how we see the world.

Jeremy Bentham was an English philosopher who lived between 1748 and 1832. His philosophy was based on the principle of the greatest happiness for the greatest number of people. He was a social reformer and radical thinker. But despite being an ultra rationalist, he was still convinced that goblins threatened his safety at night. As a result, his long-suffering assistants were made to sleep at the door of his bedroom to keep him safe from harm.

Like Bentham, our beliefs are not always rational, although we may think they are. And can lead to some eccentric behaviours. Once set, they can take some shifting. So adopting – and entrenching – the Four Autonomies Mindset to give you back control of your life may not be a walk in the park.

It's difficult to admit that we suffer from boxed thinking, and we really should get out more. This, for people of more mature years, may be exacerbated by a fear of the future that can induce a kind of mental sclerosis.

If you've been in solid employment for most of your life, it may not initially be comfortable taking the first steps towards a mindset that majors in *autonomy*. First, because many jobs stress *teamwork* as a key criterion for judging people's performance, and teamwork tends to make irrelevant any need or opportunity for autonomy.

And second, many highly demanding jobs have an emphasis on keeping up with, or beating, the *competition*. What the competition is doing now or may do in the future drives everything. While we may think we are being proactive, it can often be the fear of what our competitors might get up to which drives our thinking and behaviour.

So while your working life may have steered you round any sharp or difficult decisions pertaining to your own life – the fact you're (still) reading this book would suggest you're ready to change that.

As a Second Biter, operating in a challenging and fluid environment can be a fresh experience. You won't have a team around you to give support and encouragement. And you won't have competitors – or a demanding boss – to set the pace, or the agenda. Suddenly you are on your own, with just your historical mindsets for company.

Changing your attitude to be open, positive and proactive – to embrace autonomy – might well be hard. It could involve changing your mental models/attitudes in ways that alter not only the opportunities you see, but also the way you process the information to spot, and respond to those opportunities. It will likely impact how you respond to new people in the light of those opportunities.

Ultimately it will pave the way to embrace the Four Autonomies Mindset. Our lives so far may not have set us up with all the perspectives we now need to take control of our future but this chapter should be going some way to helping you change that.

THE GROWTH MINDSET AND THE FIXED MINDSET

Some personal development books ring bells so loudly that you just know they have hit the bullseye bang in the centre. *Mindset* by Carol Dweck, a professor of psychology at several prestigious US universities, is such a book. As you read it, you just know, both intellectually and emotionally, that it is simply right.

Its proposition is that we have two possible mindsets: a growth mindset and a fixed mindset. The preferred one is the growth mindset.

The essential difference between the two is the attitude to failing. For the fixed mindset, if you fail at something, it means you are a *failure*. For the growth mindset, if you fail at something, it just means you are *learning*. For the Fixed Mindset, if you end an enterprise that's not working, you've given up. For the Growth Mindset you're being proactive and simply going to try something new.

The good news is that because we are not permanently rooted in either, we can change to the growth version. It will not only unleash our potential, but also take away much of the stress – and potential knocks to our confidence – associated with the fixed version.

The commensurate danger, of course, is that it is also possible to move the other way. As people age there is a tendency for this to happen. This challenge will be addressed later in the chapter. For now, let's look at Dweck's work in a bit more detail.

THE FIXED MINDSET

The fixed mindset is often brought about unwittingly in people whose proud parents intended to increase their child's self-esteem by constantly telling him or her that they were brilliant.

Unfortunately, this can have the unintended consequence of their child believing it, and assuming that because they are naturally brilliant no further effort is required. Indeed, they come to believe that effort is a sign of a lack of natural talent and brilliance. Dweck's research showed over and over again that praising a child's intelligence harmed both their motivation and their performance.

Yes, someone with a fixed mindset believes effort is a very bad thing. The very fact they are having to try hard means they are a failure masquerading as a naturally talented winner. In tests, children who have a fixed mindset will turn down the opportunity to do a more difficult puzzle, and will do the easy one over and over again to avoid the possibility of failing at the harder one.

Children, and adults, with fixed mindsets believe that everyone is born with a certain level of intelligence, and not much can be done to change it. All they need to do is to validate their high level of intelligence by demonstrating their natural talent. They instinctively feel that if you have natural ability, learning is an unnecessary chore you needn't bother with.

And they look for partners, and even friends, who will put them on a pedestal and tell them they are wonderful (like their parents did).

Unfortunately for people with a fixed mindset, they seldom fulfil their potential because they believe they already have. They are the academics or sportspeople that you knew at school or college who were stars destined for glittering futures. And who were never heard of again.

Part of the inability – or unwillingness – to learn by people with a fixed mindset is exacerbated by their speed to blame others for their failure. It can't have been their fault; they have no faults (and are terrified of them). Once the blame game starts, the capacity to learn disappears immediately.

Their mind closes to any opportunity to learn from mistakes. Why bother, when it is plainly someone else's fault? Their mind closes to opportunities to try new and challenging things – the fear of failure is too big and painful a risk.

THE GROWTH MINDSET

People with a growth mindset, on the other hand, tend to have been similarly encouraged as children by their parents, but for their *effort* rather than their talent. They seek to learn, to develop. They welcome difficult tasks, because they will come out wiser, even if they fail in the short term. Being stretched is meat and drink to them.

Effort isn't proof of not having enough talent: it is evidence of eagerness to learn and grow. Failing isn't failure; it is learning. To be told something is difficult is the greatest stimulus possible for the growth mindset, whereas to the fixed mindset, it is a signal to lose interest.

Failure is still painful, but not the end of the world. You deal with it, learn from it and move on to the next failure.

Growth mindset people are not afraid to put in lots of effort, even if it may not be cool to do so. They don't mind if the effort shows, because they would rather accomplish the task in hand, however difficult, than avoid the effort merely to evade the possibility of failure.

Effort is both the friend and the raison d'être of the growth mindset. Whereas the fixed mindset is about performing, the growth mindset is about rehearsing, learning and improving. The satisfaction lies in the growth and the fulfilment of potential. Intelligence and talent aren't fixed entities – they can be developed and built upon, brick by brick.

Dweck's research also showed that people with a growth mindset deal better with depression. By consistently making the effort to do the things that looked daunting due to their condition, they did not go so far down in their depression, and emerged from it again much earlier.

The concept of a growth mindset is easy to understand, and the benefits are both apparent and significant.

But if you think you recognise yourself in some of the descriptions of the fixed mindset it can be a challenge initially to shift yourself out of it and into a growth mindset. The instinct to become frustrated if you can't immediately rise to a challenge and succeed without too much effort may not be easy to overcome. The feeling of powerlessness when you should be feeling powerful through the rapidity of your success can take time to master.

Dweck uses an enlightening metaphor to explain the process of changing from one mindset to the other. She says it's not like surgery. You can't cut out your disabling beliefs like a worn-out hip or knee joint, and replace them with new and better ones. You have to allow the new beliefs to take their place alongside the old ones, until they are developed enough to take over.

Mindsets aren't things you can pick up or discard as the whim takes you. Belief systems you have been living with perhaps for decades may need some shifting but the effort is justified by the reward.

If you are reading this book to find ways of developing more of your potential, you are already on the road to a growth mindset. You are open to learning, and you are keen to grow. Importantly, you understand you are not the finished article (the delusional and destructive comfort zone of the fixed mindset).

Intellectual humility is a very good starting point for developing new mindsets.

WHY SECOND BITERS NEED TO HAVE YOUNG BRAINS

Back in 2009 I had the privilege – and a lot of fun – writing a book with Chris Middleton called *You Can be as Young as You Think*. Chris is a behavioural scientist and futurologist; he had run a market research company in the UK which tracked social trends across Europe.

The idea underpinning the book was that we all have three ages. The first is our Birthdays Age – how many years we have been alive. The second is our Body Age – which can, according to scientists, vary fifteen years either side of our Birthdays Age, depending on how much exercise we take, our diet, whether we smoke or not, and so on (remember Blue Zones in Chapter Seven). The third age is our Brain Age. Our Brain Age is dependent on attitudes to life in general, which, of course, go to make up our mindset.

So you could have a Birthdays Age of fifty-six, a Body Age of forty-two and a Brain Age of seventy-five. Or a Birthdays Age of seventy-eight, a Body Age of eighty-three and a Brain Age of thirty. The goal, of course, is to get your Body Age a good ten years below your Birthdays Age, and your Brain Age significantly below that.

The research carried out across Europe was clear on the general trends of what we defined as our Brain Age. As people pile on the years they tend to become more conservative in their approach to life. They close down, and cease to be the fun, energetic, excited people they were in their youth.

For example, answering the attitudinal statement 'I would like to experience new feelings every day', 73 per cent of 18–24-year-olds agreed that they would actively search out new emotions, whereas only 36 per cent of those aged sixty-five+ said they would. To 'I like to have a good time in a crowd', 74 per cent of 18–24-year-olds agreed they liked being in crowds, while only 29 per cent of the sixty-five+ group felt good in crowds.

Confronted with the statement 'I feel full of energy', 53 per cent of 18–24-year-olds agreed, whereas only 29 per cent of those aged sixty-five+ did. The research, which took in a large sample over several years, and covered all the age groups between fifteen and sixty-five+ years, demonstrated two significant points:

1. Attitudinal ageing begins on nearly all dimensions from nineteen years – yes, *nineteen* onwards, and continues through the age cohorts.

2. On nearly all dimensions, a hard core of approximately 30 per cent of people aged sixty-five+ are still up for it.

We called this 30 per cent Young Brains, and the rest Middle-aged or Old Brains. The Young Brains (whether nineteen or ninety years old) exhibit consistent characteristics in their approach to life – their mindset.

THE YOUNG-BRAINED MINDSET

The good news is that you are still in control of the attitudes you adopt, and how you think. Unlike your Birthdays Age, or your Body

Age (where you can only turn the clock back fifteen years), you can have the mental approach of someone of twenty-five years old. The age, as a second biter, you probably still feel yourself to be.

Carefully examining the research evidence of how young people approach life – their attitudes and behaviours that were most effective in coping with life as it is now lived – Chris and I came up with what we termed the Six Wisdoms of Youth.

Let's be clear. We were not suggesting that youth is wise in all its aspects. Indeed, some of its attitudes and behaviours are pretty damned unattractive. The self-centredness, the selfishness, the lack of gratitude, the monosyllabic boorishness would make life hell if everyone adopted them. But certain of their behaviours are very relevant responses to modern society. They are effective coping mechanisms that work better when dealing with challenges than the way older people deal with them.

Of the Six Wisdoms of Youth, I will touch on just two here …

ADAPTIVE NAVIGATION

Adaptive Navigation describes the behaviour of young people towards the rapidity of change, which could helpfully be adopted by people who are older. While the young fix clear objectives, they are far more relaxed about the plan to get there.

Indeed, quite often they don't plan. If you have teenage or slightly older children you will recognise the pattern. Even if they have planned far enough ahead to book a ticket to get somewhere, they won't start packing till they are on the point of leaving. Winter or summer takes them entirely by surprise. They borrow each other's clothes to find something suitable.

They zig and they zag, but they get there in the end. With so much change going on all the time, they take the view instinctively that something will turn up, so don't fret about the details. To them, too much planning is boring, wastes energy and is likely to end in frustration. So go with the flow, and enjoy the journey.

Adaptive Navigation assumes that life will get in the way, so enjoy shimmying your way towards your goals, and when change happens, relax and capitalise on it. And if the goals aren't reached, no worries – find some new ones moving in a similar direction and go for those instead.

Being truly open to change – and even enjoying it – takes a huge amount of pressure and anxiety out of life. There is no need to worry – let alone get angry – about how things are going. It also acknowledges the complexities of life today. You can be at ease with ambiguity.

It does not, however, mean losing your moral compass. You still know right from wrong, and act accordingly. It just means you move away from a self-righteous position often embraced by older people – I'm right – you're wrong; it's black and white; the world's going to hell in a handcart.

It means asking yourself the question, 'What if I am wrong about this?' And then being honest in your answer. Being open to other views means you are exposing yourself to doubt. The certainties that were comforting in the past aren't there any more.

The huge benefit of Adaptive Navigation is that it avoids rigidity. You are freed up to be more flexible. Your openness means you can adapt rapidly to new situations and see in them new opportunities. You can apply energy to creating the future, rather than defending or justifying the past.

It means that you can capitalise on a changing environment, rather than being fearful of it. And you can start to trust people more. You can understand that most people are well intentioned and are not deliberately perverse or stupid.

And the biggest benefit of Youth's Wisdom of Adaptive Navigation is that you feel instinctively in tune with what's going on. You no longer feel stressed by fighting against the flow of events and how people are thinking and feeling around you.

There are lots of ways you can start on the journey to Adaptive Navigation. Basically, it's about consciously becoming more open, and more street savvy. Take a simple example. When you next buy a piece of electrical equipment, do what young people do. Read the safety warnings and then throw away the instruction manual – it's often written in gibberish anyway.

Try to make the thing work. Take risks. You'll find it's far more intuitive than you thought. You'll get it going in less time than you think. And you'll have avoided the stress of having to decipher instructions not written in a language that humans can understand.

DESIGNING TOMORROW

This is the second Wisdom of Youth I will touch on. This wisdom is about the belief that the future can be created, and we should in no way assume we are powerless in the face of events to influence outcomes.

Young Brains have the capacity and desire to hang on to their powers of imagination and invention. They resist the combination of teaching methods, syllabuses and the relentless demands of daily life to compress and stifle their powers of envisioning the future. They retain their childlike creativity and sense of what is possible.

They want both to foresee the future and to shape it.

'Younger generations … want to be in control of their lives … want to extend their sense of authorship from how they design their living rooms to how they conduct their careers, to feel autonomous, take the initiative and be rewarded with a sense of achievement and recognition.'

– Charles Leadbeater, *We-Think*

At first sight this may seem to go against the logic of Adaptive Navigation – going with the flow and letting serendipity take its course. But it's not contradictory because young people can discriminate clearly between the strategic and the tactical. The strategic – their future, and how they live – is carefully thought about, and energy is put into bringing it to fruition. The tactical – dealing with life as it comes – can be dealt with adaptively, without rigidity or getting anxious and fussing about it.

Creativity is a joy for Young Brains. Dreaming is part of their life, and the imagination is in constant use. They are free of the backward-looking, constantly hankering after the past Old Brain thinking that denies any role for creativity: the feeling of why be creative, even if I could be?

Alain de Botton, in *Essays in Love*, defines this syndrome as *psycho-fatalism*. These Old-Brained people are 'bewildered and exhausted, because they suffocate on question marks: Why me? Why this? Why now?'

Creativity – in all its glorious manifestations – music, gardening, painting, writing, cooking, how you dress, solving problems, how you freshen and enliven relationships, finding new ways to give back, or to grow, just playing, finding new ways to earn money – is the stuff of life to the Young Brain.

Getting yourself into a Young Brained mindset where you *can* create your own future as well as a life rich in imagination and invention may need some application. We are all creative, but may be a bit rusty in using our creativity – and it can be a bit daunting to take the first steps. But there are tools to do the job.

Being optimistic is a powerful start.

Being pessimistic is a non-starter if you want to be creative, or indeed do anything worthwhile. Pessimism freezes any inclination towards creativity, and it induces a false sense of helplessness. Pessimists believe nothing they do will alter the outcome of life around them. They are paralysed by their own sense of ineffectiveness. In psychological studies, pessimists are found to achieve less, give up more easily and get depressed more regularly.

Optimists may sometimes believe things are better than they really are, but they still get things done, create things, and inspire others to do likewise.

Inventing magic is another approach to encouraging and developing creativity. Creating magic moments for children or grandchildren – and enjoying them as much as they do – is a fun way to get the creative juices flowing.

And putting aside time – on a walk, a plane trip, in a chair you seldom use – is an effective way to get dreaming again. Romance and enchantment can be fun. Old Brains, especially male Old Brains, can struggle a bit with this. But hang in there. Dreams stimulate creativity and can lead to some interesting situations.

IT ALL COMES BACK TO AUTONOMY

Young Brains are by nature people with a mind of their own. Autonomy comes naturally to them. They are adaptable, resourceful, flexible, and they respond creatively to the world as they find it.

They have enthusiasm, energy and enjoy creating magic. Why wouldn't they want to be in control of their own lives?

So ensuring you have Young Brain attitudes, *and* have a growth mindset, is a very good starting point in developing your autonomies.

And owning the autonomies – really taking hold of your current and future wellbeing – is a great starting point to taking your second bite of the cherry.

GET YOUR MOUTH WATERING FOR YOUR
SECOND BITE OF THE CHERRY

Let's consolidate what you might have learned in this chapter:

1. For confirmation that many prejudices about society going to the dogs are a myth, go to Perceptions are not a reality on ipsos-mori.com/_assets/sri/perils. You'll be surprised at what you find.

2. Read *Mindset: How You Can Fulfill Your Potential* by Dr Carol Dweck. An eye- and mind-opener.

3. Discover your Brain Age to find out more about your openness to mindset change. There's a Brain Age Test early on in the book *You can be as Young as You Think* by myself and Chris Middleton, or go to the free app: Brain Age Test RevelMob

Ideas to explore this element further:

1. 'This is hard. This is fun' – once you hear yourself saying this according to Carol Dweck, you are well on the way to a Growth Mindset. Repeat the words, and apply them, until you believe them.

2. Take a look at the TED talk of Elizabeth Gilbert (author of *Eat, Pray, Love*), entitled *Elizabeth Gilbert: Your elusive creative genius:* ted.com/talks/elizabeth_gilbert_on_genius

3. Revisit the classic Ken Robinson TED talk on the natural creativity of children, and how schools bludgeon it out of them: ted.com/talks/ken_robinson_says_schools_kill_creativity

CHAPTER NINE

FINDING COURAGE AND MEANING ON THE JOURNEY

'Man's reach must exceed his grasp, or what's a heaven for?'

– Robert Browning, 'Fra Lippo Lippi'

**SEVEN INSIDIOUS EXCUSES FORCEFULLY REJECTED
BY HIGHLY EFFECTIVE PEOPLE**

EXCUSE NO.7

I'm comfortable. Just about. There are significant downsides to trying to reinvent myself as a Second Biter. Why risk failing?

Not to give it a go is just mediocre. And you'll die not knowing whether you could have had a rich and fulfilling new beginning, in which you would really start to come alive.

Before you launch yourself on your fresh and exciting trajectory, this chapter will arm you with a final few tools, approaches and mindsets to help you on your way and ensure you can reap the benefits of the Four Autonomies.

Your journey has begun but it is unlikely to be smooth and bump-free.

Stuff, as we know, happens. So there will be setbacks. And you will need courage to overcome them. And as a Second Biter a little extra courage might be needed to overcome the nagging sense of thwarted entitlement which intensifies the pain of the setbacks.

This sense of thwarted entitlement comes from realising that as we get older we have not accomplished the great achievements – and perhaps the financial wealth – that we always thought we would. It is brought into sharp relief when things go wrong – even relatively small things. We might say to ourselves 'I'm X years old. I've been relatively successful. Done a lot. I've earned some respect. I have a place in the world. How can this indignity be happening to me? It's unfair. I deserve better.'

Sorry, but the rules of life don't change because you've reached a certain age. Pratfalls and embarrassments will occur frequently – especially if you are truly in control of your own destiny and are taking some risks to make new things happen.

Getting outside comfort zones incurs discomfort. Fact. You can't gently edge your way to the new and exciting you. It needs the odd risk to be taken, and with risk comes the possibility of failure.

So, courage is needed on the voyage.

FINDING MEANING SUPERCHARGES EVERYTHING

'The two most important days in your life are the day you are born and the day you find out why.'

– Mark Twain

Mark Twain's famous quote goes to the heart of it. If you can find meaning in what you are doing, all the difficult stuff shrinks into insignificance. It means those bumps and pratfalls are far easier to bear.

Some of us have always known what they wanted to do. If you are one of those lucky people who are doing it now, congratulations. And if you've always had a burning passion to do something but never have, well, The Second Bite is ready and waiting for you. Go for it!

But most of us wrestle with that big question – what is my calling? Instead we find *meaning,* a feeling that what we are doing is worthwhile, and chimes strongly with our values and beliefs.

It is closely linked to purpose, the words often used interchangeably, and it can be just as powerful a motivator. They are interrelated, one usually generating the other, and there's no rule as to which comes first. Knowing your purpose can bring meaning to your life. And equally, finding meaning in what you do can lead to a clarified purpose. Whichever comes first, ultimately they both lead to *fulfilment* – a sense that you know why you're here and what you're here to do.

Finding your purpose is a tricky thing (I recommend a few of the many books on the subject at the end of this book), while finding meaning in what you do, though not always easy, is more straightforward. With that in mind, here are one or two more thoughts on finding meaning that might help.

'Artists are pilgrims on the road to meaning.'

– Grayson Perry, British artist

The majority of us have a hunger for a world that is fairer and better and we want to help contribute to achieving that. In a confusing universe we have a yearning for significance and meaning. The search for meaning is a quest that touches us at a profound level.

We look for meaning in our work and often can't find it, which prompts us to look elsewhere.

In the West, this search for meaning probably comes from four main areas:

- **A lack of simple-to-grasp issues that unified society in previous generations.** External threats bring people together as a society and gives them purpose. Fighting Nazism or apartheid or racism gives people meaning. Unifying against a glaring evil is straightforward. Fighting religious extremism of all sorts is hugely important, but today it is so varied, and so geographically disparate, that it is less easy for an individual to get a handle on at a local level.

- **Because many of us in the West (with the notable exception of the United States) nowadays do not have strong religious faith, it is a less powerful provider of meaning than in previous generations.** The subsequent withering of the moral framework that goes with this loss of faith has led to a void in people's lives, whether recognised consciously or not. The reduction in shared belief systems and sense of mutual responsibility provided by religion can leave people disorientated.

- **Rising affluence in the West has removed the common purpose of work.** Putting food on the table for ourselves and our loved ones is easily covered, where once it provided a strong, shared incentive to the work we were doing. We've also got over the excessive consumerism of the twentieth century; an extra car gives no real buzz either. Today, *experiences* excite us more than *things*. While a brilliant societal development (in the developed world, at least, we're making and buying less unnecessary stuff), leaves us bereft of a common meaning – what qualifies as an exciting experience is not something widely shared.

- **A strong driver in our desire for meaning is that it can counter stress and anxiety.** Life is uncomfortably pressurised, but if it has meaning it is more worthwhile to make the effort to cope with it. Meaning turns stress into positive energy.

So materially comfortable but stressful lives, coupled with no overwhelmingly important battles we can easily engage in, has left us with a slightly guilty feeling that we need to have a larger cause to fight for. Especially if our job has been one that is challenging but not fulfilling.

As we saw in the Giving Autonomy, activism for a good cause, or volunteering to help fellow humans in need, or contributing to the improvement of the environment all engage us actively. We are creating direct, targeted value in each case, and our reward for that creation of value is finding meaning and fulfilment.

But it needn't just be through exercising our Giving Autonomy that we balance our lives.

As I mentioned in Chapter 5, the **way I've found meaning and a subsequent purpose is by** *making a difference.* It's simple. I feast on the mutuality of benefit that comes from helping others while getting a buzz of meaning and a sense of purpose out of it myself.

Whether it is writing, chairing chief executive think tanks, being a trustee of various charities, or getting involved in some front-line stuff for those charities, all the aspects of what I do are both stimulating and rewarding, and involve mutual benefit. There's some difficult stuff involved, but that is good because I am challenged and I'm creating value for others by overcoming those challenges.

The experiences that the West now hankers after, rather than material goods, has seen a huge rise in gallery, museum, festival, concert and sports participation. We are touched and involved in the particular experience because it gives us pleasure (recharging us), engages us at a profound level, brings out more of our humanity and because we feel it has meaning and significance. But while we bring ourselves to them in an open and generous way, we are doing more taking than giving. We feed on what they give us, but we play little part in their creation.

When you open that café you've always wanted to do to take charge of your Earning Autonomy, or perhaps it's the sculpture studio you've finally got off the ground in your Recharging Autonomy – to give it meaning you'll want to weave in value creation (Giving) there too. It might be that your café hosts the luncheon club once a week for the local elderly. Or that you open your studio up to teach some kids once a month. Or it could be as simple as the joy your warm welcome brings your customers or the beauty your pots bring to their owners.

What you'll also start to notice is that by finding that balance between giving and taking across your autonomies, you'll find meaning in everything you do. All four of the Autonomies will start firing together. You'll see a thread of purpose running through them all – they start reinforcing each other – all sustained by a balance of giving and receiving. It's an ecosystem that once going, will be hard to stop.

You may need to scratch a lot of itches to find fulfilment, but find it you will. It is unlikely to arrive in a neat and simple form – it may show itself as a common theme to various activities and not necessarily as one you can describe simply. Others may not fully understand you, but once you have found fulfilment, your natural enthusiasm will carry you through. You will find not only purpose and meaning but also a passion to change things for the better.

'Work is about searching for daily meaning as well as daily bread, for recognition as well as cash, for astonishment rather than torpor, in short for a life, rather than for a Monday through Friday sort of dying'

— Studs Terkel, *Working*

POSITIVE STEPS WILL BEAR YOU ALONG

We all have an inner voice that continually whispers negative thoughts in our ear. Yes, that negative inner voice which tells you you're not good enough, you won't succeed, and it's not worth it. It's the voice that articulates the Seven Insidious Excuses you need to reject in order to be a Highly Effective Person. And there's a whole lot more than seven.

It's the voice behind the Imposter Syndrome that tells you that you are about to be found out at any moment. It's the voice that needs to be told to shut up whenever it starts its whispering. But victory over it is never complete, and never permanent.

There are many ways to keep the voice quiet, and we have touched on several in previous chapters. A major defence against its negative blandishments is your continued personal and psychological growth, which is why the Learning Autonomy is so important.

Having a purpose, and finding meaning in what you are doing, is, of course, another powerful muffler of the insidious purveyor of self-doubt. Beyond all this, it's worth recognising that we are all human and we need to work on our self-esteem. So, classic personal development and positive-thinking techniques are a valuable part of your armoury.

Having, and exercising, the Four Autonomies – of Earning, Learning, Giving and Recharging – will supercharge both your personal growth and your psychological development. The autonomies will re-frame your mental model and give you a larger comfort zone. And ultimately they will give you a new understanding of yourself as a Second Biter. Someone who is going to grab retirement or redundancy by the horns and make it work for you.

But while autonomy is vital, it is no guarantee of instant bliss. No one has total control over outcomes. We need to be brave and recognise that we have the power to act and to shape our stories. We need to step up and take responsibility for the extent of the ripples travelling outwards from our lives that shape events both for ourselves and for others. And we will need courage to overcome the hurdles along the way. Starting the journey will make us stronger; it will get easier the further we go.

A LITTLE HELPER

However assiduous our work on personal development may have been, there are times when we could do with a little more help. When you are scared, you're scared, and having some aid to hand can be mighty comforting.

What I use is an NLP (neuro-linguistic programming) technique to shore up courage. If the need arises, I become what I call a **Mighty Lion**. Daft as it sounds, it works.

The theory is that we have *enabling states* and *paralysing states*. Enabling states are states where we feel confidence, joy, love and inner strength. Paralysing states are those during which we feel anxiety, confusion, depression, fear and low self-worth.

Our behaviour tends to be a direct result of the state we are in. If something makes us feel afraid, and we are in a paralysing state, we are in even bigger trouble than we need to be, because we can't even think straight. So the ability to get ourselves rapidly into an enabling state can come in very useful.

To develop this ability you need to create what is called an *anchor*. An anchor is a sensory stimulus linked to a specific state – similar to the bell that got Pavlov's dogs salivating. (The Russian psychologist had programmed them to expect food every time the bell rang, and when the food was removed, they still salivated at the anticipation of the non-existent food.)

To create your anchor, you select a physical gesture – say, crooking your little finger – and then pre-construct a whole battery of positive feelings associated with it. To do this, you select four or five experiences in your life when you felt empowered to a very high degree. This could be taking part in a sporting event, playing a solo part in a public event, being applauded for a speech, being honoured for an achievement at work, or just being thanked for an act of kindness.

Whatever the events you select, it is important to relive them with all the colour, sounds, smells and emotion of the event itself. While you are programming the anchor (do it with full concentration, ten times), it is helpful to sit upright or stand up, with the chest out, so the body mirrors the pride you are feeling at reliving the moments of triumph.

Once you have programmed them into the selected anchor – by reliving them while pressing the crooked little finger or whatever you select – you can start to mine the benefits. When you are in a low or paralysed state, just make the selected gesture. Then feel the sense of confidence and empowerment sweep through you.

My first experience of using the technique somewhat backfired. Not because it didn't work: it worked only too well.

I was on a long training run for my first London Marathon, and was getting towards the end of a pretty gruelling outing. I had about a mile to go before I could stop, have a breather and generally recover. My pace became even slower as the tiredness began to overcome me.

Suddenly, my stride lengthened, and I began to speed up. The discomfort of such effort for that last mile was considerable. I was out of breath and distressed to a degree more suitable to an Olympic Final than a gentle training run.

I finally arrived at my front gate. Exhausted. And baffled. I looked down and saw the culprit. In the state of physical discomfort I was suffering at the end of the run I had clenched my fist. In doing so, I had dug my thumb into my anchor finger, setting off my Mighty Lion response.

I was relieved to know I could be a Mighty Lion if I needed to, but was careful to keep the powerful beast caged on subsequent training runs.

LIFE EXPERIENCE BRINGS REAL BENEFITS

Your life is a well of confidence to draw from. It will enable you to cope with the majority of what re-engaging in life as a Second Biter can throw at you. *So it is important not to undervalue that experience.* Not only should you not undervalue it, you should, wherever possible, capitalise on it.

You should look for every opportunity to increase your value to others by leveraging your experience and insight. As well as getting rewarded for that experience, rather than just for your time – it can be much more satisfying, and is a win/win for all concerned.

So when you're thinking about **giving** (beyond financial giving), you find projects where you can add significant value beyond the time you spend on them. This can be in terms of helpful connections that can supercharge your contribution through expertise or access to funding.

And when you are thinking about **earning**, you look for projects where you don't only get paid once. You create or develop an asset, and get paid for as long as it lasts. If a project involves a wider team, try to ensure the key players all benefit long term as well, as it develops longevity.

I learned this lesson early in my career as someone without a conventional job. I was in a position of financial vulnerability, but I was intensely aware that I didn't want to work directly for anybody else, whatever was on offer.

So, I have tried to do work that generated repeat business as well as work on specific projects for immediate financial rewards. I did, and still do, one-off work. But I have also been lucky enough to create assets that still require work but have longevity, which means I'm not continually reinventing the wheel.

The think tanks I run have endured for more than twenty years. For me personally, the benefits are simple. Apart from the income, which is moderate but regular and very welcome, I learn a great deal from the speakers invited in to rattle the cages of the members and get them thinking beyond last week's sales figures. And I also like the members. I learn from them and very much enjoy sharing their company.

So it's worth thinking hard about how you could create such assets. It means you can build a core of engaged, enthusiastic customers with whom you are in regular contact. It reduces the number of cold calls you will need to make and sparks relationships. And most importantly of all, it means you will find more satisfaction in what you do, as well as having more confidence doing it.

YOUR BRAND

This may seem a strange notion if you are not planning to set up a company, but communicating who you are, and feeling confident in that communication, will be a great way of anchoring your identity and building trusting relationships with the new people and projects you may choose to give your time to.

Communicating who you are and what you can offer is always a challenge, but building your personal brand is a useful approach. You may no longer work for X company or organisation, which, whether you were aware of it or not, was an important part of your identity. Now you work for Brand You.

Everything you do, in all your areas of activity, contributes to Brand You. The brand may not yet have a high saliency in the outside world (though you are building it day by day), but it constitutes who you are. Which is why you should behave with integrity at all times. Integrity means being the same honest person in all situations.

Not for you the situational ethic, where circumstances determine who you are and how you behave. Integrity is thus the source of your self-esteem, your trust as a brand and your value as a human being.

Building your brand is a large subject, and there is insufficient space to deal with it here. There are some suggestions at the end of the book on where to find more insight.

Suffice it to say, it could be very beneficial to remember that the choices you make with your various autonomies will all contribute both to your identity (who you know yourself to be) and your branding to the outside world.

It would be unwise to dismiss the idea of your personal brand. All brands are about trust. You buy them because you know their provenance and your experience of them is positive. They deliver consistently and reliably. Your brand is the same. The trust you build up increases the likelihood of a customer – or a donor, if you are working with a charity – coming back again and again.

As a good brand, you will be continually updating yourself. You will be trusted because you are not only experienced and you deliver, but because you are a continually learning and sharing wisdom. People will be happy to hear from you. They will know you are creating new value, not peddling the same old, same old.

And in today's connected economy you will be continually building your own personal assets and brand. You won't be an employee building someone else's.

This is especially relevant given the rapid development of peer-to-peer rating.

User-generated feedback systems mean there is transparency on your qualities as a buyer – or a seller – of a service. If you use Uber or Airbnb, for example, you will be rated on your performance as a provider of a service or, if you use it, as a user. Just as you are with eBay.

The trust rating of your brand will thus be available for all to inspect. There is no hiding place. Peer-to-peer rating systems tend to improve the overall standards in a market, as poor service to consumers, or poor behaviour as a consumer, is quickly apparent for all to see.

So your personal brand is under a spotlight as never before. This provides an unprecedented opportunity to excel – and be recognised as excellent.

IT'S YOUR SONG, NOT KARAOKE

The joy of the Four Autonomies is that they give you control of all the aspects of your life – and how they fit together. You will be singing your own song. And if you want it to be, it can be a new tune, in a new key.

Put another way, you are no longer shopping in IKEA for a ready-made pre-pack of how you obtain your income, where or how you choose to give back, where you decide to develop your professional or life skills, or where you choose to recharge your batteries. You can select your own pieces and assemble them in the way *you* want.

You can choose how you work, with whom you work, at what you work and when you work. *And you can choose your own balance of autonomies*. Your work may not involve earning at all. It may be voluntary, and be part of your Giving as well. Your Learning may come in bursts, or it may be regular. It's up to you: you are in control.

The balance of your autonomies is likely to change as events impact upon your life. Recharging, for example, may occur at different times across the year, and may involve no work, or earning, for a period of time. One constant will be the creation of new value, which will become an intrinsic part of finding meaning and achieving fulfilment.

The Four Autonomies are not discreet boxes. They overlap and evolve over time. The crucial thing to remember is that all four have a part to play in your life, and if any of them shrivels too much, you are in danger of shrivelling yourself as a human being.

The key to it all is that you are in control of who you are and what you do.

The time for boxed thinking is over. You're outside the box, and you're free.

CHAPTER TEN

MARCHING ON TO VICTORY
AS A SECOND BITER

'To dare is to lose one's footing momentarily.
Not to dare is to lose oneself.'

– Soren Kierkegaard

So we've reached the last chapter, and it's time to get on with it.

Let's quickly look at the ground we have covered so far. We understand that to avoid a future that is worrying financially, as well as being unchallenging and unfulfilling, we need to positively take control of our lives. This involves being autonomous in the four areas:

Earning to keep us solvent and in touch with the world.

Learning regularly and actively to keep developing as human beings.

Giving back socially and/or financially, as it's a win/win thing to do.

Recharging to make sure we're relaxed, stimulated and full of energy for our other autonomies.

And not forgetting to exercise **Enlightened Thrift**, in order to value what we have, and be ready, if necessary, to have less.

DARING TO DREAM

Second Biters are pioneers. We are leading the charge for new ways of working and living when society expects us to just go quietly into retirement followed quickly by the care home. We have never lived in a time with so many older people, in such good health, with so many opportunities.

You will be part of the team leading the way, reinventing how redundancy or retirement is lived. It's no longer a given that you'll settle in and wait to die.

Conventional jobs will still exist going forward, but they will be for conventional people. You have the opportunity to innovate a new way of working, thinking and giving back. And finding fulfilment in doing so.

'Those who danced were thought insane
by those who could not hear the music.'

– Friedrich Nietzsche

The Four Autonomies and the concept of being a Second Biter have come together from observations, lived experience and inspiration from many clever thinkers. Broken down, the concepts are not new – but pulling them together will give us the power and framework to redefine how we can cope more effectively with the opportunities and challenges that changes in society are throwing up.

I find that incredibly motivating. And more so that subsequent generations of children and grandchildren will benefit from our learnings and achievements. It could well be a LEGACY to the young.

'Traditional societies tend to be materially poorer, but socially richer. Loneliness in old age is unheard of.'

– Jared Diamond, polymath and author of *The Third Chimpanzee: the Evolution and Future of the Human Animal*

Autonomy is essentially selfish. It is about gaining individual control. We live in a society which is atomising – each separate particle putting itself and its interests first. The Four Autonomies take advantage of that atomisation. The difference is that as part of Generation Cherry you will be putting that autonomy to positive use. You will be looking to live a life that is socially richer.

The essence of being a Second Biter is that you create social value. You have seen enough of life to appreciate that true satisfaction and fulfilment come from using all your skills to enrich others. It is a form of self-interested selflessness. You benefit. Your clients or customers benefit. Your family benefits. And society benefits. It is the ultimate win/win. This is a big goal, and will require courage.

Small dreams are easily overcome by fear. And it's too easy to be busy, busy. Being busy protects you from having big dreams and pursuing them. Willpower and guts are the foundation of every realised dream.

So let's get down to business and take some action.

PLAN OUT YOUR LIFE CARD (AND GET SOME PRINTED)

Your Life Card is a step on from your business card. It is a card you can hand to someone you meet, whom you find engaging and with whom there might be mutual value in staying in contact.

The major benefit of a Life Card over a business card is that it gives the person receiving it an insight into who you are as a person and a human being. It also gives them reason to question you further so the conversation can become much richer. Your Life Card will provide much more fertile ground for discussions with people you meet, as well as giving them a much clearer idea of who you are. It provides a bit of backstory on you as well as stimulus for further interesting dialogue.

This is an opportunity to create your own palette. Experiment with a few versions of yourself until you find something you are comfortable with. You'll probably find it takes a few iterations until your personal version of a Second Biter crystallises.

You will notice that your Life Card contains no previous job titles. No past president of this or emeritus professor of that. This is because it is about **who you are**, not **who you were.** It is about your current identity, which contains your skills, enthusiasms and learnings. It's not about one or two fancy titles you may have picked up along the way.

To give you an idea of how yours might work, here's mine. It's printed on two sides.

SIDE ONE

The final slash on side one is helpful. Most people I give my card to crack into a smile at the 'All-round Good Egg'. It takes away any pomposity, and lightens the tone all round. Have a think about what phrase you could use to achieve a similar effect.

The last two lines on that side are crucial, too. It's so easy to have a stack of cards you have been given by people you found interesting at the time, only to look at them a few weeks later and find you haven't a clue where you met, what you talked about – indeed, anything about them. I find including a photo of yourself is helpful, as it helps people remember what you looked like.

And putting your description as 'Second Biter' will give a further stimulus to fruitful conversation. As will side two…

SIDE TWO

EARNING:	Speaker, Writer, Think Tank Chairman.
LEARNING:	Humanising business; Meaning and Fulfilment.
GIVING:	Active Trustee: RAHAB (helping people trafficked into the sex trade); Romilly Forshall Foundation (supporting street children in Africa), Miliffe Scholarship Fund (very small – helping developing world scholars). Prison mentor for 20+ years.
RECHARGING:	Family, sport & fitness, reading, theatre, travel.

That's a brief summary of who I am. It covers my Four Autonomies and gives a much fuller picture of how I approach life.

In a sense, your Life Card becomes a mini, but relevant CV. It describes both who you are, and *some of the growth points on your journey to today*. But be careful of putting anything on your card that sounds like a boast. Any implication that you are special, or superior in some way, is not a great way to start a dialogue – an important reason for having the card in the first place.

The content of your Life Card is entirely up to you and it may take several attempts before you find one you are happy with.

You may not want to describe yourself as a Second Biter. Perhaps you're a Senior Slasher. Perhaps you're not. It's up to you. But it's worth developing a card along these lines, even if you never get it printed, because it helps to define your current identity. You will feel more confident in who you are, even if you don't choose to go public with it at this point.

Here are some ideas to think about. It's far from exhaustive – just a prompt to encourage you to create your own Life Card. There will be infinite ways of making sure your strengths, interests and expertise are covered, so be creative.

EARNING:

Business development

Commercial, Family law, etc.

Translating

Sourcing funds

Non-exec work

Project management

Management

Leadership development

Developing social projects

Woodwork

Engineering

Interim management projects

Plumbing

Electrical work

Enlightened Thrift Specialist

… and so on

LEARNING:

Law

Accounting

Creativity

Start-ups

Angel investing

Finance

Art

Business projects

Creative projects

Music

Mentoring

Non-exec directorships

Teaching	Horticulture
Medicine	... and so on

GIVING:

Social projects	Wealth creation (social,
Mentoring	economic, learning)
Teaching and Education	Volunteer
Pro bono work	... and so on

RECHARGING:

Soul nourishment	Languages
History	Astronomy
Leadership	Travel
Management	Culture
International Development	Sport (golf, tennis, etc.)
Piano	Sudoku
Geology	Reading
Painting	Yoga
Sculpture	Drawing
Computer science	Music
	... and so on

THE CHOICE

We have reached decision time. Will you continue as you are or will you become a Second Biter? For me, it is a no-brainer.

A word cloud is a device to give emphasis to the elements contained within a concept. Let me present a couple of subjectively assembled word clouds to crystallise the choice.

OPTION ONE: THE NON-BITER'S WORD CLOUD

Accept a life of poodling on and sinking into a pleasant, unthreatening twilight of your life. A twilight that might last for more years than you want, and end up losing all excitement, stimulus and fulfilment.

No sweat to achieve – just do nothing, and hope something turns up.

OPTION TWO: THE SECOND-BITER'S WORD CLOUD

This is where you smile, take control of your life and go for it.

As I say, a no-brainer.

AUTONOMY MEANS FREEDOM

Becoming a Second Biter means you will leave behind even the possibility of becoming a member of the living dead.

You will become more fully alive and you'll write a new, exciting and fulfilling chapter in the story of your life.

There are plenty of examples of people who left their flowering till late in life. Alfred Hitchcock made the majority of his most memorable and iconic movies in his late fifties and early sixties. Degas, Cézanne, Van Gogh, Miles Davis, Goya, Monet, Lina Bo Bardi, Robert Frost, Agatha Christie, Theodor Seuss Geisel and many others were all at their most productive – and most creative – in later years. As were Verdi (he wrote *Falstaff* at seventy-eight) and Sophocles (he wrote *Oedipus at Colonus* at eighty-nine).

> Pablo Casals, the world-famous cellist, was asked in his nineties why he kept practising. He replied: 'Because I'm making progress.'

These great artists give us the evidence that we, in our more humble but still worthwhile and potentially significant way can live stimulating and fruitful lives. We all age, and with increasing age comes challenges. We can resist it for a time, but to pretend it doesn't happen is daft. If we do that, we give up the chance to develop – to learn and grow. And in doing so, we give up the chance to be fully human. Fundamentally, ageing is a success.

The Four Autonomies give us the chance to take control, so we can at last be free. Free to say no if we don't feel what is being offered or suggested is right. And free to fulfil ourselves by continuing to grow as human beings.

The future is a positive and exciting territory. As a Second Biter you have talent, time and kindness to give. Your example will be an inspiration to others. They in turn will aspire to and fulfil more of their potential.

Best of all, you will be more alive. And because the more you give the more you live, your talent, wisdom and enthusiasm will help to create a better future for all concerned. And you will be able to wholeheartedly celebrate being part of it.

To be a part of Generation Cherry is a privilege and a blessing. The opportunity now is to move on to become a Second Biter. Another privilege and another blessing. So, open your mouth. The sweet, juicy cherry of life is once more in front of you. Bite it; relish it. It will energise and delight you.

FURTHER READING
AND VIEWING

Here are some reminders of things to think about and places to look for inspiration and support on each area outlined in the book:

Whatever you do or don't do when you've finished this book, make sure you sign up to websites like the thersa.org/discover/videos and ted.com/talks.

Then look at the Do Lectures website: thedolectures.com/talks If you have time, watch one by a young fellow called Tim Drake in 2012.

Make it a regular part of Wisdom Wednesdays (see Chapter 5), or use it as a companion when travelling.

ENLIGHTENED THRIFT

Read, or re-read, Stephen Covey's *The 7 Habits of Highly Effective People* to examine the Abundance Mindset and the Scarcity Mindset in more detail. The book is a treasure trove of wisdom.

Read *Rich Dad, Poor Dad* by Robert Kiyosaki. There's some stuff that may not be directly relevant, such as how the US tax system affects financial planning, but the core of the idea is brilliant.

Check out Tim Ferriss's five-minute talk for Google where he touches on Seneca Stoicism as a huge source of perspective to rebalance his fears: youtube.com/watch?v=88Ui_nflxka

'Poverty is a description of someone's economic situation; it does not describe who someone is' – a quote from Jacqueline Novogratz of Acumen. Take a good look at their website: acumen.org. It will help you accelerate the sense of proportion that comes with Enlightened Thrift.

EARNING

While you are looking for your core income stream(s) (which might take a bit of time), dabble in alternatives to find one or two that might suit you:

- selling your excess clothing, accessories, jewellery and furniture on Etsy or eBay
- Save money by car sharing on BlablaCar
- monetising your home on Airbnb or onefinestay
- selling your expertise(s) on TaskRabbit.

LEARNING

Watch How to Find & Do Work on liveyourlegend.net. Scott Dinsmore was a young American who was excited by the idea of making work meaningful and enjoyable. He absorbed the teachings of the wise personal development teachers of the past, and absorbed them well.

Sadly, he died in a freak rockfall while climbing Kilimanjaro, but his legacy lives on, supported by his widow and friends around the world.

Start honing your purpose. Go to the free website howtomakeadifference.co.uk and start working on your Values Map and your Living Legacy.

Start your Mastermind Group: six–eight people is good; two–five is OK. To find one online, simply type in 'Mastermind Group' and see what the internet has to offer.

Try taking a self-funded sabbatical or two to work for a period as an intern. Choose an organisation in which to get a feel of whether a particular line of work might be suitable for you.

Find a Muse or two.

If you have an idea of a new or existing area of work, search out people already working in that sort of area. Talk to them. Ask questions (work them out in advance). People are usually generous with their time and keen to help.

For further reading on Purpose, read Ken Robinson's excellent book *The Element: How Finding Your Passion Changes Everything*.

If you are mature in years, take a look at the University of the Third Age. I haven't myself explored its benefits, as I am fully engaged across the spectrum of autonomies, but any organisation that has as a slogan 'Learn, Laugh and Live!' has to be worth a look: u3a.org.uk

GIVING

Think about the ways in which you will give: will it be Volunteering, Philanthropy, Recognition of Others, or General Goodness? Or a judicious combination of all of them?

Volunteering can be inconvenient. Try to make sure that within this constraint you concentrate on consciously feeling autonomous, in control. Giving away too much autonomy could be counterproductive.

RECHARGING

Read André Aleman's *Our Ageing Brain* to reassure yourself that most of your marbles are still there, and operating more or less effectively.

Comb the section in this book on *Cognitive recharging: soul nourishment* and make **two lists:**

1. The first will be fresh activities you haven't tried in years (sketching, meditation, breathing exercises, visiting an art gallery). Determine to do as many as possible in the next three months.

2. The second list will involve doing three things you have never tried and which are slightly outside your comfort zone. Do at least one of these in the next six months.

If you are prepared for some heavy lifting on mindfulness and spirituality, take a look at Eckhart Tolle's *The Power of Now*. It contains some powerful wisdom, including how and why to avoid negativity.

If you want some helpful tips to get through the internal voices discouraging you from getting started at a creative passion you have left dormant, *The War of Art* by Steven Pressfield is worth a look. It paints a good picture of the mental hurdles and how to jump them, as well as developing your chosen passion into a more serious professional pursuit if you want to take it further.

COURAGE AND MEANING

1. Read *Man's Search for Meaning*, written by Viktor Frankl, a psychiatrist who was imprisoned in Auschwitz and lived to tell the tale. He concluded that the ones who survived the longest were those who took back autonomy and comforted others, sometimes giving them their last crust of bread. A great book.

2. For great insights on purpose and leadership do read *Leadership from the Inside Out* by Kevin Cashman. A deserved classic.

3. Read, or re-read, some of the personal-development classics to work on your character and your courage (we all need to). Start with *The Magic of Thinking Big* by David Schwartz and *How to Win Friends and Influence People* by Dale Carnegie (yes, worth reading. It's deservedly a classic).

YOUR BRAND

Watch Rachel Botsman's TED talk on 'reputation capital', the Currency of the New Economy is Trust, to understand some of the new parameters of personal branding going forward:

ted.com/talks/rachel_botsman_the_currency_of_the_new_economy_is_trust

Read *Brand You: Turn Your Unique Talents into a Winning Formula (Financial Times Guides)* by John Purkiss and David Royston-Lee, for the elements of and an approach to personal brand building.

ACKNOWLEDGEMENTS

Life Mentor: Lizzie Drake

Book Mentor: Tansy Drake

Muses: muses are sometimes regular, sometimes occasional, inspirers. Some are like old friends that you may not see for a long period – years even - but you when talk to them, you pick up again as if it were yesterday. Here are some of mine:

Charles Kingsmill
Richard Gibson
Michael Townsend Williams
Chris Middleton
David Pearl
Seth Godin (even though I've never met him)

Agent: Adrian Weston, a support and inspiration over many years.

Publishers: the fantastic team at RedDoor. In particular Clare Christian and Heather Boisseau, who make publishing such a positive and enjoyable experience.

INDEX

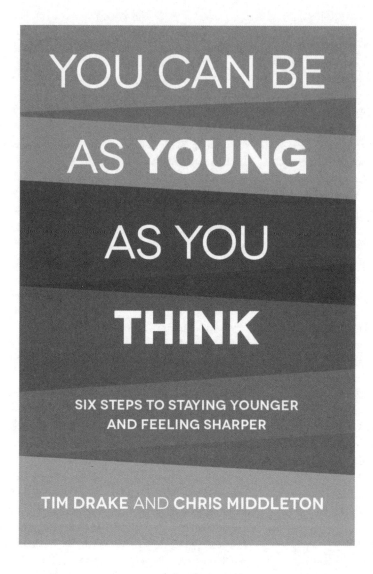

YOU CAN BE AS YOUNG AS YOU THINK

AS **YOUNG**

AS YOU

THINK

SIX STEPS TO STAYING YOUNGER
AND FEELING SHARPER

TIM DRAKE AND **CHRIS MIDDLETON**

YOU CAN BE AS YOUNG AS YOU THINK:
SIX STEPS TO STAYING YOUNGER AND FEELING SHARPER
(e-book edition)
£4.99
Available for download from January 2017 from
all distribution channels including iBooks and Amazon.

ABOUT THE AUTHOR

Tim Drake has co-founded and run businesses, think tanks and charities. He is a keynote speaker to business audiences around Europe on personal and group motivation, and unlocking potential.

He believes that he, like most people, has more to give. He also recognises that setbacks are part of life, and to make progress we need insight into what sort of journey we are on and why we are on it. Plus a sense of humour to make sure we enjoy the serendipities along the way.

Now in his seventies, he is still sees himself as a promising youngster setting out on new adventures.